The author

Edinburgh-born Graeme Cornwallis, who aspires to know Scotland inside out, studied astronomy at Glasgow University and later travelled the globe in search of mountains to climb. His travels took him to all the inhabited continents and, with a solid knowledge of travel, tourism and hiking, he wrote or contributed to many guidebooks for the backpacker's favourite, Lonely Planet – including the guide to Scotland. When he is not hiking or writing, Cornwallis teaches mathematics and physics at home in Glasgow.

Pure Mental

Graeme Cornwallis

Fort Publishing Ltd

First published in 2004 by Fort Publishing Ltd, Old Belmont House,
12 Robsland Avenue, Ayr, KA7 2RW

Printed by Bell and Bain, Glasgow

Cover illustration and text cartoons by Andy Hammond

Graphic design by Mark Blackadder

Typeset by S. Fairgrieve (0131-658-1763)

Thanks to the staff of the Mitchell Library, Glasgow and
the National Library of Scotland, Edinburgh.

ISBN 0-9547431-1-3

Contents

1

Clerical errors

Priests, ministers and nuns are there to set the rest of us an example. A very bad example.

Drunken priest fondled housekeeper's breasts

It was one of the most embarrassing episodes in the history of the Roman Catholic Church in Scotland. He was a much-respected priest, albeit with a drink problem. She was a busty, wannabee topless model with a chequered past and a reputation as a loose cannon. So when Father David Brown gave Maria McBride (31) a job in his chapel house it was an accident just waiting to happen.

He employed her as his housekeeper at St Thomas's church in Riddrie, Glasgow. As might be expected, she was far from the traditional image of a priest's housekeeper and often dressed in high heels and short skirts. But Father Brown (48) had known Maria since she was 8 years old and he was a close friend of her devout Catholic parents. Perhaps he reasoned that she would get back on to the straight and narrow while in the presence of the Lord.

But he was soon to regret his decision, and found himself in court on six charges of sexual assault and breach of the peace involving Maria and two other women. She said it all started when one of her female friends stayed in the chapel house one night in October 1997. She said that she saw the priest – who had drunk almost a full bottle of malt whisky – come out of her friend's bedroom when the woman had very little on.

Then, when McBride herself was asleep, she claimed that Father Brown came into the room and woke her up. 'He lay on the bed and fondled me' she recalled, 'It was like a nightmare. I

Maria McBride

pushed him away. He told me he loved me and that he was a virgin and that if he ever had sex he would want to do it with me.' In other incidents she said the priest cuddled her, sometimes touching her breasts or putting his hands under her clothing. On another occasion he held her face in his hands and tried to kiss her.

It was alleged in court that McBride had only made the allegations when she saw how much he was drinking and became worried he would be moved and that, as a result, she would lose her job. She also said that she was sacked by Father Brown despite personal assurances from the leader of Scotland's Roman Catholics – Cardinal Thomas Winning – that her job was safe and that he would get help for 'Big D' (the Cardinal's nickname for Father Brown).

Father Brown was found guilty of one charge of sexual assault and three charges of breach of the peace at Glasgow Sheriff Court. Sheriff MacIver said his offences were at the lower end of the scale and admonished him. But perhaps the most interesting facts to emerge in the aftermath of the case concerned Maria McBride, described as having a hysterical personality disorder by her own psychiatrist:

- She had three children to a married Pakistani she first met at the age of 15
- She was paid £8,000 to marry a Pakistani waiter to help him stay in Scotland
- She worked as an erotic dancer in a gay club
- She sent nude photographs of herself to newspapers in an attempt to become a Page Three girl
- She sold her story to a tabloid for £12,000 before making a complaint to police about Father Brown
- She made false allegations of child abuse against her babysitter
- She faced eviction from a council flat after allegations of brothel-keeping were made against her by neighbours

McBride also took the priest to an industrial tribunal claiming sex discrimination and unfair dismissal; the case was settled out of court. As for Father Brown, he was moved to another parish.

1999

He thought the bubbles would cover it

Staff at the exclusive Crieff Hydro Hotel couldn't believe their eyes. One of their guests was playing with himself in the jacuzzi. And to make matters worse Robert Hugh Drummond was a man of the cloth. As one worker explained: 'We could see clearly what he was doing but needed to be certain so we turned the bubbles off and watched from a window. The water went down instantly and he was caught with his shorts down, trying desperately to cover his private parts.'

The randy rev, who is in his seventies, had been a regular visitor to the hotel for years. He said, 'I thought you would not be able to see anything because of the bubbles. I am very sorry if I caused offence by my actions as I didn't mean to.' Despite a discreet warning from the management Mr Drummond – a locum minister from Edinburgh – planned to go back to the £300-a-night hotel, where clergymen get a substantial discount.

But he faced the possibility of disciplinary action by the Church of Scotland, which intended to investigate once all the facts were known.

2004

Priest told off-colour joke

Father Paul Friel, a priest at St Ninian's church in Knightswood, Glasgow shocked his flock with the following joke about a Rangers player. It was around the time that Rangers manager Walter Smith signed Basile Boli, a Frenchman of African origin. Basile did not distinguish himself at Ibrox.

The joke was:

Walter Smith was charged £1.5 million for a fish supper at his local chippie. When he complained the owner said, 'Why complain? You've just spent £2.7 million on a black pudding.'

Unfortunately for Father Friel several members of his congregation were not amused and complained to the Roman Catholic hierarchy in Glasgow. Through the diocesan office the red-faced cleric apologised and said that it was not his intention to offend anyone.

1994

He was no saviour

The congregation at Uddingston's Park parish church, which included dozens of Cubs and Scouts, was listening intently as Revd Earlsley White gave a sermon about a friend who had died for his faith.

Suddenly, a man dressed like an SAS soldier in balaclava, combat gear and with a blacked-up face burst in. Brandishing a gun, he frogmarched the session clerk, Craig Mains, to the front of the church. The masked man shouted 'this is not a fucking joke' and forced Mr Mains to his knees. He blindfolded the minister and told him he would kill him if he did not renounce his faith. He bundled Revd White out of a side door and the stunned churchgoers then heard two pistol shots.

This caused panic in the church and, understandably, many in the congregation feared they would be shot. But then the minister reappeared and told the congregation, 'That is what happened to my friend. He was killed for his beliefs. His name was Jesus.'

The youngsters in the church were particularly shocked by the incident; many were in tears and some were hysterical. After all, it was only a year since the massacre at Dunblane primary school when Thomas Hamilton murdered sixteen children. The police also took the whole thing very seriously and sent an armed unit to the church after receiving a 999 call.

It turned out that the gunman was former SAS corporal Matthew Smith and that he and Revd White had cooked up the stunt between them to illustrate the sermon. This cut little ice with the authorities and both men were prosecuted for breach of the peace at Hamilton Sheriff Court. Revd White was fined £500 and Smith, who had eight previous convictions, got 240 hours community service.

1998

Missionary position

Reverend Helen Percy was feeling sorry for herself. She was lying in her bed with a dose of the flu. As a single woman, she was alone in her little cottage in the remote hamlet of Kilry, Tayside. So she must have been pleased when kindly neighbour Sandy Nicoll called to bring her hot soup. And she was probably even more pleased when he jumped into bed and had sex with her.

After rumours of an affair leaked out she was suspended from her job as an associate Church of Scotland minister, and faced the prospect of being sacked. So Percy did what any resourceful liar would have done: she changed her story. She had initially admitted having consensual sex with Nicoll, a married Kirk elder. But then, in a complete about face, she claimed he raped her. She even went for rape counselling and claimed that she let Nicoll have intercourse with her because of the trauma of being abused in her childhood.

But her story was blown apart when Nicoll's wife released an explosive letter from Percy to her husband. It read: 'You must insist that you did indeed rape me when I was ill in bed . . . I can't stop loving you or forget the pain and tenderness we have shared – and could share again if we are very patient and very careful – and for fuck's sake don't leave any more bits of paper, receipts, incriminating evidence lying around.'

Details of Percy's eccentric lifestyle began to emerge. In a previous posting – to Paisley of all places – neighbours got up a petition to make her get rid of her pets: Vietnamese pot-bellied pigs. She also took convicted murderer Andrew Smith home for three days at Christmas 1995 when he was on a week's leave from his life sentence. And, in a stunt that led parishioners to call her a witch, she gave a church sermon in her nightie. This, apparently, was to demonstrate that it did not matter how people appeared before God. Percy also aborted Nicoll's baby in 1997.

Percy resigned from her post rather than face a church court but then, true to form, she launched a series of legal actions that included hearings at an industrial tribunal and the Court of Session. When both were rejected, the Church of Scotland set up a special panel of experts in 2003 to examine her claim that she would have been better treated if she had been a male minister. The panel also rejected her claim. It is understood that Percy may now take her case to the House of Lords.

Helen Percy is now a missionary in South Africa. She is no doubt a shining example of Christian values to the 'heathens' she is trying to convert.

1997 and 2003

The Sash their father played

Father Sam McGinness stunned the congregation at St Mary's RC church in Irvine, Ayrshire when he played Orange anthem, 'The Sash', on his harmonica. The Irish-born priest also told a Rangers supporter, 'Your team was lucky yesterday.'

The church was packed with Catholics and Protestants celebrating Marymass, a non-denominational community event. Father McGinness said: 'We have to forget about the prejudices of the past and look to the future.'

1992

Hell's Angels on highway to heaven

Scots-born churchman and former Govan shipyard worker Paul Sinclair (37) set up a funeral service for motorcyclists – with a specially adapted sidecar hearse to take bikers on their final journey. Nicknamed the Faster Pastor, Paul gave up regular work as a Pentecostal church pastor to concentrate on funerals for bike fans. He studied designs for traditional Jaguar and Daimler hearses for months before he built the prototype sidecar for his firm Motorcycle Funerals Ltd, which is based in Leicestershire.

The first sidecar hearse, which cost around £450 to hire, was built onto a Triumph Cafe Racer bike and won the 'Best Modern Hearse' award in the Hearse of the Year competition 2003. A second sidecar hearse was attached to an even more powerful 1298 cc Suzuki Hayabusa. Astonished police held up one funeral, and the DVLA later created a new vehicle classification: the two-wheel hearse.

Mr Sinclair said that funerals should reflect the lives of the deceased and the company website adds: 'For a dignified final ride. Available for non-religious, religious, slow, fast and very fast funerals.'

2003

Airheads die on fresh-air diet

On 16 September 1999, Verity Linn (49) was found dead just one hundred yards from her tent, pitched near Cam Loch in Sutherland. Her body was mysteriously curled in the foetal position and she was wearing only a waterproof jacket, which was pulled-up over her head. Her diary was found in the tent, and had references to a cult called Breatharianism. There was also a disturbing book entitled *Living on Light*, which contained the teachings of self-proclaimed prophet Ellen Greve, an Australian woman whose beliefs brought her five thousand followers and a luxury mansion in Brisbane. Greve preached that we could survive from light and the air we breathe and claimed that she had survived off virtually nothing for five years. Of course, these beliefs have never stood up to scientific scrutiny.

The cult's initiation ceremony consisted of fasting for twenty-one days: no food or drink for the first seven days, then only sips of water for a further fourteen days. But poor Verity, an Australian, failed to complete the course. She worked as manager of the educational centre at the Findhorn Foundation, a New Age organisation and had travelled to Sutherland after two days of fasting. She thought that Greve's programme would spiritually cleanse her body and 'recharge her both physically and mentally' before the year 2000.

In an already weakened state, she walked over a mile to a beautiful spot overlooking the loch. It is thought that she got up at night to go to the toilet during wet and cold weather but could not find her way back to the tent. Due to her recent lack of sustenance, she quickly died of hypothermia and dehydration around eight days into her fast. The post mortem revealed that she had not had a drink for at least two days and stated that lack of nutrition was a secondary cause in her death.

While some friends defended Verity Linn's hotchpotch philosophies – including crystal therapy, Buddhism and meditation – educationalist and former Findhorn Foundation member John Paul Greenaway attacked the community and claimed that its teaching made followers 'susceptible to dubious philosophies'.

Ellen Greve, whose husband is a convicted fraudster and serial bankrupt, was exposed as a fake on Australian television when she was unable to follow her own 'air diet' for even a few days. And in November 1999, Breatharian fanatics Jim Pesnak (61) and his wife Eugenia (63) were convicted in Brisbane of the manslaughter of gullible 53-year-old Lani Morris. The Pesnaks, jailed for six and two years respectively, encouraged Morris to follow the air diet for eleven days but she died from a severe stroke, kidney failure, pneumonia, starvation and dehydration.

1999

Nun too good

Following a sensational court case, nun Marie Theresa Docherty, also known as Sister Alphonso, was found guilty of four child-cruelty offences, with three others not proven, while working at Nazareth House orphanages in Aberdeen and Lasswade, Midlothian. The indictment listed twenty-three offences, covering a fifteen-year reign of terror dating from 1965. Docherty – who sat in court dressed in a full nun's habit – denied all charges. During the trial, she was accused of:

- Hitting children with a hairbrush and other implements
- Swinging a child by the hair
- Force-feeding a youngster with vomit-covered food
- Making others wear urine-soaked pants on their heads
- Smashing a girl's head against a radiator
- Forcing frightened girls to kiss a stinking corpse
- Subjecting bed-wetters to cold baths

In court, Docherty (58) justified severe discipline by saying that, when a child, she asked her father to use a belt on her bare bottom because she deserved a leathering.

Despite her appalling crimes, Sheriff Colin Harris admonished Docherty due to her age, a heart condition, lack of previous convictions and the length of time that had passed. This prompted one victim to shout: 'Why don't you give her a box of chocolates, too?' As Docherty walked to freedom, she was attacked by vigilantes who bombarded her with coins and spat at her.

Furious victims condemned the sentence as a joke and the farcical trial at Aberdeen Sheriff Court was said to be a 'complete waste of taxpayers' money'. Many took the view that she got preferential treatment because she was a nun.

During Docherty's trial, her lawyer claimed that angry residents at Nazareth House (by then an old people's home) opposed the court proceedings and wanted her back. He also argued that the prospect of compensation cash had encouraged people to come forward.

Following the trial the Roman Catholic Church seemed to be in denial about the degree of abuse in their homes. Mario Conti, then Roman Catholic bishop of Aberdeen and Orkney, said that Docherty had 'glowing testimonials'. Conti later claimed that Docherty was innocent and that her conviction should be quashed. In March 2003, he even nominated a lawyer who had come out of retirement to work on the defence case for a Papal knighthood for his commitment to the Church.

In fact, the Docherty case was only the tip of the iceberg of alleged violence within Roman Catholic orphanages. Many other victims claimed to have received or seen beatings at Lanark's Smylum Park and the Nazareth House orphanage in Cardonald, Glasgow. One man described how a violent nun at Smylum Park bashed him on the head with a crucifix and that his wound required stitches. Another resident said that a nun at Cardonald almost strangled her and battered her in the face with a spade. Lawyer Cameron Fyfe had lodged compensation claims against the Catholic Church in the civil courts totalling £8.5 million

2000–2003

Brownie pack

Married Church of Scotland minister Revd Campbell Ferenbach seduced brownie leader Jill Warwick in 1961 when she was 17 – and fathered her five children in a secret affair. The truth was discovered when Ferenbach's deathbed 'confession letter' was opened by mistake. The cheating minister made a recovery but his wife Alice, the mother of another three of his children, booted him out after fifty-six years of marriage and nearly twenty-five years of lies.

Ferenbach, who ministered over Edinburgh's Liberton parish

for twenty-eight years, married Jill Warwick at the ripe old age of 80, only two years after fathering her fifth baby. She described Ferenbach as a 'weak-minded man', said that he was never a proper father to her children and claims she was 'just a bit on the side'. While ex-wife Alice revealed that Ferenbach, who she divorced a year after the affair became known, never said he was sorry.

In the 'confession letter', Ferenbach justified his behaviour by claiming that Jill would never have married anyone else and that he fathered her children to save her from childlessness, saying the 'moral burden of his irregularity' was 'almost unbearable'. He died aged 90 in February 1995.

1995

2

The law is an ass

Many of our elderly population are easily confused and frequently baffled by the decisions taken in our courts. They are called judges.

Aye couldn't help it

It may have been the solemnity of the proceedings in Stirling Sheriff Court that overwhelmed accused man, Kevin Mathieson. But he could not bring himself to utter the 'yes' word.

- Asked if he was indeed Kevin Mathieson, he replied 'aye'
- When Sheriff James Nolan told him he must reply either 'yes' or 'no' Kevin again said 'aye'
- Advised that he would be held in contempt of court if he did not say either yes or no, and if he understood the potential punishment, Mathieson of course replied 'aye'

At the end of his tether, Sheriff Nolan sent Kevin to the cells. He was brought back later and apologised. Mathieson was in court for falling behind in paying the instalments of a £120 fine, which he agreed to bring up to date. He was not charged with contempt of court.

Scots language expert David Murison said the sheriff's decision was quite preposterous as 'aye' is standard Scots.

1993

Silly old barrister

He had no doubt heard the word somewhere. But Sheriff Donald Booker-Millburn wasn't sure if calling someone a 'poof' was an insult or not. So he asked defence lawyer Gordon Addison, who duly enlightened him.

On trial in Inverness Sheriff Court was John Worthington-Flitcroft (53) who had been driven out of Kingussie after a campaign of harassment by local youngsters who:

- Taunted and ridiculed him
- Threw stones and snowballs at his windows
- Baited him with cries of 'fat poof' and 'poofter'

One day when he was out for a walk with his 19-year-old boyfriend, Mr Worthington-Flitcroft lost the plot. When two girls called him a poof, he slapped them on the face. He admitted the assault and was ordered to pay the girls compensation of £75 each.

1991

A misleading case

The use of DNA testing cleared a man of incest. He had been jailed for two years in 1986 for having sex with his lawful daughter between 1982 and 1985. He was released after a year but was again charged with having sex with the girl in 1988.

At that point a DNA test was carried out and it revealed that the 49-year-old man from the Borders was not the girl's natural father. And, as she was over 16 in 1982 when they first had sex, he had committed no crime. In 1990, the Court of Criminal Appeal quashed his 1986 conviction, describing the case as 'highly unusual'.

1990

Raped . . . then charged

It was probably the most shameful prosecution in the annals of Scottish criminal history. A case that even now beggars belief.

It all started when a 19-year-old girl was raped in a car park in Dalkeith, Midlothian. A brutal attacker left her lying unconscious, naked except for her shoes. When the unfortunate young woman woke up in hospital she thought she was being attacked again. Confused and frightened, she spat at a doctor and struggled with police who were trying to hold her down. She later explained: 'I don't remember anything about attacking anyone or spitting . . . I didn't want them to touch me. I just wanted my mum.'

A decision was made to charge her with these 'offences' and she was hauled before Edinburgh Sheriff Court. Her lawyer, Nigel Beaumont, said he was astonished at the decision to prosecute and noted that she had twice tried to commit suicide since the attack.

The woman admitted the charges and Sheriff Peter Ballance deferred sentence for six months for good behaviour. She was eventually admonished.

Understandably the woman was embittered by the whole affair. She said: 'I wish now I'd never complained about the attack. The way I've been treated, it is as if I was to blame.' She was no doubt also angry that, at the time of her court case, no one had been apprehended for raping her.

There was a happy ending of sorts. Six months after her ordeal in court she revealed that she and her boyfriend were expecting a baby and they planned to marry.

1990

A glaring error

An Ayrshire man probably thought things couldn't get any worse. He had just seen his two brothers jailed at Kilmarnock Sheriff Court; one for twelve months and the other for thirty months. They had been involved in a disturbance at a house in Saltcoats during which a policeman was threatened with a gun.

But what happened next really put the tin lid on a bad day. He was given six months in jail for giving the jury an evil glare.

Sheriff Terence Russell took the view that his glare amounted to contempt of court and he was hauled back into court by police as he left the public gallery. The 26-year-old dad was remanded in custody for six days before being sentenced.

His girlfriend was enraged: 'The sentence is a disgrace. People walk free for stabbings and much more serious crimes.'

1996

Heads or jail

Robert Gavin must be the unluckiest – and most gullible criminal – of all time. Along with accomplice Sean Padden he was on trial at the High Court in Glasgow on armed robbery charges in connection with a raid on the Clydesdale Bank in the city's Laurieston area.

The robbery had been a farce from start to finish. As they fled with their ill-gotten gains a booby-trapped parcel of money exploded and stained them and the cash with red dye. Witnesses then saw them make off in a Volvo, alerted the police and they were quickly apprehended.

In court the blundering blaggers were told that the Crown would accept a guilty plea from one of them rather than go to trial. So they trooped off to their cell to work out who would take the rap. What better way to decide their fate than to toss for it, and so they enlisted the help of fellow prisoner and murder-accused Tam Hunter to spin a coin.

Robert Gavin described what happened next: 'We decided it would be the best of five. Sean won the first two. I won the next two. I called "heads" in the last one but it was tails. I then told my counsel I wanted to plead to it because we'd shaken hands on it. My lawyer said I was daft. . . . But we had made a deal.'

Incredibly, the Crown accepted Padden's plea of not guilty, despite the fact police found evidence that he was the dominant partner in the duo's bank job. So, on the spin of a coin, Gavin was sentenced to eight years for assault and robbery and eighteen months on a firearms charge. After cooling his heels in prison for a while he clearly thought better of the deal and demanded a probe into the whole affair.

1997

A very lucrative trip

The farcical state of our legal system was laid bare by a case involving Fife man Vincent Kemp (36). He had been out on the piss with brother David, who estimated they had about six pints of beer each at various pubs and clubs.

Full of ale, the bold Vincent tripped over a raised kerb at Rosyth dockyard and was hit by a van, suffering serious head and spine injuries. He was paralysed in the accident and now faces life in a wheelchair.

Kemp decided to sue the secretary of state for Scotland, who was responsible for maintaining the pavement. His number came up seven years later at the Court of Session, when he was awarded £500,000 compensation. Kemp would have got £750,000 but the judge, Lord Osborne, ruled that he was partly to blame because he had been under the influence of alcohol. He also ruled that the raised kerb, which was hard to see in poor light, carried a reasonably foreseeable risk of injury.

Although the decision caused outrage in many quarters, Kemp was unmoved by the criticism: 'I am very happy with the result of the amount of money' he said. He also believed it would make life safer for pedestrians. Vince, your humanity is a lesson for us all.

1999

An ugly incident

In a judgement at Perth Sheriff Court, epilepsy sufferer Edwin Young was ordered to pay compensation to Yvonne Rennie.

She claimed to have suffered post-traumatic stress after seeing Mr Young's contorted face during a fit. Sheriff Michael Fletcher ruled that damages should be paid because 'the image of his face upset her', despite suggesting the woman may have exaggerated her symptoms. The decision, which highlighted the extremes of our compensation culture, was widely condemned and Epilepsy Action Scotland described the ruling as 'bizarre'.

Mrs Rennie, of Perth, took court action following an accident in 1998 when Mr Young ran into the back of her car at traffic lights following an epileptic attack. He admitted responsibility for the accident and was ordered to pay £1,500 compensation for her minor physical injuries.

However Mrs Rennie – who thought Mr Young was dying from a heart attack – claimed she had been deeply disturbed by the look on his face as he lay on the pavement, after passers-by had pulled him from his car. Sheriff Fletcher awarded her a further £3,500 for stress related to seeing the fit, plus £1,000 for private counselling to deal with a driving phobia she developed afterwards. This was despite the fact that psychiatrists had disagreed in court on whether she actually suffered post-traumatic stress disorder. The court also heard she was treated before the crash for suspected depression and chronic-fatigue syndrome.

Mr Young's pithy observation following the case was: 'She can get stuffed.'

2002

Is that Kung Fu?

When a student nurse went through his martial arts routine in the car park at Crichton Royal psychiatric hospital in Dumfries, little did he know that in a few minutes he would be arrested, charged under the Mental Health Act and spend months facing the threat of prosecution.

All the staff at the hospital knew that Grant Steele (34) was a licensed martial arts expert, except for a new receptionist who panicked and called police when she saw an 'armed man'. Despite protesting that he was a nurse, Mr Steele was surrounded by cops who used a loudhailer to demand he dropped his weapons, which turned out to be blunt, aluminium T'ai Chi swords.

The hapless nurse was hauled off to Dumfries police station in handcuffs and charged. He was then fingerprinted, DNA samples were taken and his tutor at Bell College of Nursing was asked if he had shown evidence of mental illness. Police also contacted a consultant psychiatrist from Crichton Royal, who advised them that he was completely sane. Mr Steele was released, but the procurator fiscal did not drop the case for five months, by which time the nurse's studies had been badly affected by the threat of jail and the loss of his job.

1999

Streak of bad luck

Former Royal Marine Steve Gough (44) became a celebrity during his seven-month hike from Lands End to John O'Groats – wearing only a bush hat, rucksack, socks and hiking boots.

Known as the naked rambler, the crusading naturist's bizarre aim was to promote public nudity as acceptable behaviour. He was arrested for walking around starkers fifteen times (four times in the Highlands), appeared in court four times and he spent five months in prison (often in solitary confinement) costing the taxpayer thousands of pounds. While in England the authorities generally turned a blind eye to his naturist trek, his progress through Scotland was not quite as smooth.

On 3 October 2003, Gough, of Eastleigh in Hampshire, appeared in Dingwall Sheriff Court wearing only a blanket. Kathleen MacDonald (52), of Tore on the Black Isle, testified that she was 'quite intimidated' by the sight of Gough outside her cottage. He was convicted of breach of the peace and admonished. Later the same day, Gough was re-arrested while strutting across the Cromarty bridge in the buff. He was remanded in custody in Porterfield prison, Inverness until his trial on 7 November, when he was found guilty of walking naked in public 'in circumstances likely to produce a road safety hazard and a breach of the peace'. Later that month at Inverness Sheriff Court, Sheriff Alexander Pollock said he could 'see no alternative to a custodial sentence' and he was jailed for three months. Gough, who appeared in court handcuffed and attired in a red blanket, said he would continue his walk when released.

The following day he restarted his trek in cold and rainy weather but had covered only three miles before he was lifted again in Evanton. His trial was set for January, so Gough enjoyed a 'Happy Nude Year' in a nice warm jail. On 7 January, Gough was sentenced to three months backdated to 1 December. Giving evidence, and despite Gough's popularity among other locals, the Evanton resident who had reported him said: 'I think there is a time and a place for it. I did not think Evanton was the place for it, or any other village.'

After his release, Gough managed to get to John O'Groats by 22 January without further interference. He was welcomed by a crowd of onlookers who showered him in champagne, followed by a hot meal and a soft bed.

However, Highlands and Islands Tory MSP Mary Scanlon fulminated over the waste of resources and said: 'It's outrageous that the Scottish Prison Service has to pick up the tab for this person. If someone wishes to highlight their human rights I don't see why the taxpayer should pay the bill.'

2003–2004

Bonny lad canna mak oot the Scots

A Geordie was excused from a jury because he couldn't understand the Scottish accent. Adrian Roberts from Sunderland was on duty at Edinburgh Sheriff Court but couldn't follow what was happening.

He said, 'I had just been sworn in and was speaking to a lass next to me when the sheriff asked if there was a problem. I told him that there was and it was agreed I could go.'

Adrian has a Scottish wife, Martha, and he had only lived in Scotland for three years. Martha confirmed she often had to act as translator for him.

1992

3

Sexy Scots

Scots don't have a great reputation for their performance in the bedroom. That is completely unjustified.

Get your tits out for the boys (in blue)

Boozed-up party girl Evelyn Stewart (33) was in big trouble. She had been caught drink driving, refused to take a breath test and was in a police cell in Levenmouth, Fife.

But the bold Evelyn was more concerned about showing her particulars. Cops found her stripped down to her knickers and doing a handstand against the cell wall. With her breasts bared she shouted, 'Look at my tits. They cost me a lot of money.' Then, when told to get dressed, she replied, 'Never mind your notepad, look at my tits.'

Evelyn, a nurse, was justifiably proud of her new boobs, which were a massive 38 HH. They cost £3,000 and were a birthday present to herself. She said it was money well spent. 'It has given me amazing self-confidence. . . . It has also done wonders for my love life, although I don't have a man in my life at the moment.' She had also received offers to model.

She regretted the drunk diving and said she was mortified at being prosecuted. She added, 'I know I've always been daft, but I guess I've always been a bit of a fun girl.'

1997

Evelyn Stewart

Beans on toes

The sheer ghastliness of Comic Relief, with its forced jollity and smug self-righteousness, is a turn-off for many Scots. But for one Edinburgh woman the 2003 event had a much more bizarre, and sinister, outcome. A man called at her shop in the New Town just as it was closing for the day claiming he was carrying out stunts to raise money for the charity. As Comic Relief day was in the offing, and he was wearing a red nose, she agreed to help. He asked her to close her eyes and to guess what he was covering her feet with. The man poured cold baked beans and a variety of other foodstuffs over her feet. He then left the shop without asking for a donation.

Later that night the woman told her friends what had happened and realised she had been conned by a pervert. She contacted the police who launched an investigation. Officers said they were anxious to find the man as he might have a foot fetish and target other women on their own. They later arrested and charged a man in connection with the incident.

2003

Puggy pervert put schoolgirls on the game

Observant customers at Alexander Gibson's Village Diner in Airdrie might have wondered how the teenage schoolgirls who hung around always had so much money for the slot machines, or 'puggies' as they are known in the west of Scotland. They would have been shocked to learn the truth: owner Alexander Gibson (48) had turned them into prostitutes to fund their obsession with gambling . . . and to satisfy his sick lust.

The seedy saga started when a 13-year-old asked him for a loan to play the puggies. Gibson was used to his young female customers asking him for money for the machines and used to laugh it off. But this time he agreed to lend her the cash – if she had sex with him. Two days later Gibson had intercourse with her. She then told her pals about the seedy pact and, before long, the depraved businessman was having sex with six different schoolgirls. Sadly, two of them were only 12 years old.

The girls often turned up wearing their full school uniform and he would close the café to make sure they were not disturbed. The going rate was £60 for full sex and £20 for hand relief. The whole operation ran like clockwork and three of the girls even took it in turns to service him on a weekly basis. Another girl, visiting the café for the first time, had sex with Gibson and was paid £50.

Amazingly the arrangement lasted for two years. The girls' parents didn't have a clue what was going on; they thought their daughters earned the extra money on a work-experience scheme in the café. The truth only came out when one of the girls told a pal. She then told her mum, who contacted the police.

At the High Court in Glasgow, Gibson admitted ten offences against six girls, five of them from the same school. His not guilty pleas to a further eleven charges – involving another three girls – were accepted by the prosecution. Lord Osborne sentenced Gibson to eight years in jail. As a police spokesman said in the aftermath of the case: 'Children of that age have to be protected, even from themselves.'

1997

Do you want to know a secret?

Saucy Caroline McLaughlan had a guilty secret. But she just couldn't keep it to herself. She had taken her knickers off at a bowling-club dance and put them in her husband's pocket.

She told the club's vice president and the bar staff that she wasn't wearing any pants. But officials at the Kincaidston and Belmont bowling club in Ayr clearly thought Caroline (43) had provided too much information and promptly threw her out of the club. She was also unable to play at any local bowling club after news of the incident leaked out. Her daughter-in-law, Elaine, had also been banned after lady members said they could see her knickers as she bent over tables.

Caroline was upset at the ban and gave her version of events: 'I was wearing quite an expensive evening dress and yes I did go to the ladies and take off my pants. I returned and put them in my husband's pocket but that is all, and surely that is between us.'

Club secretary William Fulton responded, using a phrase he probably now regrets: 'As far as we are concerned the matter is in the hands of our solicitor. We are not prepared to wash our dirty linen in public.'

Caroline McLaughlan said she intended to sue the club for damages.

1995

The lust of a lonely woman

The divorcee (27) was a sad and lonely woman. She was living in a village in Stirlingshire and had little or no adult company. Her ex-husband said that when she came round to try and patch up their marriage, 'she was desperate and offered to go upstairs there and then'. But her feelings of isolation led her down a road that would end in a prison term and national notoriety.

The woman became so desperate that she seduced two boys, aged 13 and 11. She knew them both as they often played with her own children, and she would let the boys smoke and drink alcohol in her home. In one shameful episode she sat astride the 11-year-old and forced him to touch her naked breasts. The lustful brunette then tried to have intercourse with him but failed because the boy was not fully developed. She was caught sitting naked on him by the boy's sister but told the girl to go away; she then put a wardrobe across the door to stop them from being disturbed. She later admitted performing sex acts on both boys.

She tried hard to justify her shameless conduct: 'I did it because I was lonely. I just wanted someone to touch me. It wouldn't have mattered how old the boy was. I needed to feel love and affection.'

But the courts had no time for her excuses. She was sentenced to six months in prison at Stirling Sheriff Court.

1996

Every schoolboy's dream

It is a fantasy for teenage boys all over the world. To be seduced by a sexy, experienced woman. Especially when that woman is your teacher and has put on black suspenders and stockings to lure you into her bed. That is what happened to 14-year-old Kevin Black when he met raven-haired Dorothy Gillespie.

Kevin, who was the product of a broken home, had been sent to Park View residential school in Dundee for petty crimes. Gillespie (45) was his drama teacher, and a woman with a decidedly bohemian outlook on life despite having a husband and three children. The attractive former model quickly became obsessed by him and one day, alone in a classroom, they had a serious discussion about emotions. Gillespie saw her chance and kissed him passionately on the lips. From then on they met in secret and Gillespie bombarded him with love notes.

Six weeks later she was on a course at Strathclyde University and invited him to her bedroom when he was on a weekend home visit. Kevin said: 'As soon as we got in and shut the door that was it. We had a glass of white wine and then she stripped herself off. She was wearing black suspenders and stockings. Then she took off my clothes. It was kind of frenzied and it was over quite quickly at first but we stayed up all night. We made love twice.'

The affair lasted for two years. Gillespie even went to his mother's flat and they had sex in his little sister's room while Kevin's mother lay crippled with arthritis in the next room. She was only asked to leave the school after the headmaster found explicit letters from the teacher in Kevin's room. But the relationship was far from over and when Kevin turned 16 he moved in with Gillespie to a luxury flat in Lancefield Quay, Glasgow. Soon the young man felt suffocated and realised his passion was not love, but infatuation. In a fit of pique he walked out, went straight to Park View, robbed the school and pulled a knife on someone. He was sentenced to two years in Polmont young offenders' institution.

Gillespie was still obsessed with her young lover and sent him more than two hundred letters while he was inside, many of them sexually explicit. In one she wrote, 'Darling, your fantasy with warm oils and glowing candles was just beautiful and it's such a lovely thought you rubbing my breasts with scented oils.' In another she said, 'You bring out the wild animal in me. I'm looking forward to buying a sexy outfit for you. . . . As for you sexpot you turn me on most when you wear jeans with no underwear. That makes me wild with desire.'

Her other fantasies were more imaginative. She described a scenario in which she tied Kevin to a tree and molested him. While in another letter she said she wanted to dress up in a nurse's uniform and look after him: 'You are very full of the flu and feeling tired and sleepy. . . . You close your eyes and I put on a very wicked sexy nurse's uniform. I would have to undress you because you were hot and fevered.' The letter was accompanied by a drawing showing Kevin tied to a bedpost. But Gillespie had to stop writing at that point. The reason? She was 'on fire'.

But despite the trouble she had got into Gillespie seemed insatiable and, while Kevin was in prison, she was on the lookout for another toy boy. She got her chance while receiving treatment in hospital for depression: she expressed an interest in meeting Jonathan McKenzie, the 22-year-old son of a fellow patient. They met in the hospital canteen and the young man described what happened during a walk in the grounds: 'We put our arms around each other and kissed. It was really passionate. One thing led to another and we were on the ground, tearing off our clothes. We could not get enough of each other.'

Jonathan was soon installed in Gillespie's flat in Lancefield Quay where the sex got even kinkier. He recalled what happened when the *Waverley* paddle-steamer went past: 'They got more of a sight than they imagined because we were lying naked on her big double bed . . . in full view of the passengers waving to us. It was one of the crazy things Dorothy liked to do. She was an exhibitionist. She enjoyed parading up and down the balcony naked with a glass of wine in her hand.'

When the affairs finished, Gillespie was unemployed and embarrassed to face her family. In her defence she claimed that she had fallen in love with Kevin after first feeling sorry for him. She felt that she had got carried away at a time when her marriage was going through a rough patch and her children were growing up. As for Kevin, he too had mixed feelings: 'I'm glad to be shot of her. The sex was brilliant. I am sure any red-blooded young male would jump at the chance but getting involved with her was a mistake.'

1999

Dung-porn shame of petty officer

This is a story that belongs in the 'how could they do it?' category. A sailor was caught with magazines that showed gays eating shit. A petty officer at the nuclear-submarine base at Faslane, he found out about the so-called 'scat club' in a top-shelf publication.

He was in charge of forty men at the top-secret base and his marriage had recently broken up. The magazines, which cost £20, were seized by Customs' officers during a raid on his home in Garelochhead, Dunbartonshire. The sailor (34) was found guilty of importing obscene material into Britain from Holland and fined £500 by Dumbarton Sheriff Court.

1990

The gay-sex romps of the Tartan Army

You may have wondered what the foot soldiers of the Tartan Army get up to when they travel abroad. That is, apart from dressing-up like buffoons and singing infantile songs from the *Sound of Music.*

The truth came out in the holiday resort of Albufeira as Scotland fans partied ahead of a football international with Portugal. The debauched scenes included:

- Scottish fans stripping off and cavorting nude in the streets.
- Tartan Army footsoldiers playing football naked in a park.
- Drunken fans roaming the streets singing, shouting and swearing.
- Men standing in the middle of the road and lifting their kilts while they had nothing on underneath.

But the most shocking incident of all occurred in a bar. Owner Manuel Brandao saw one fan lift the kilt of a companion and perform a sex act on him. Although Mr Brandao was convinced they were doing it for a joke, as was his barman, they could see that some onlookers might have been offended.

The Portuguese police obviously thought so and arrested two Midlothian men. The courts took an equally stern view of what had happened and sentenced them to five months in jail. But they served only two weeks after their families met the prime minister of Portugal, Mario Soares, who was visiting Edinburgh.

1993

Phone sex gave him the pip

Bob and Jessie Grant of Grangemouth were heartily sick of their bonking neighbours. If they could just have done it in their bedrooms, and not in the BT phone box 12 yards from their house. As Jessie explained: 'We can't park our cars there because they throw used condoms on the bonnet. You can even see their bare backsides against the windows of the box. Sometimes the girls sit on our fence and have sex with the boys.' Bob and Jessie had asked British Telecom to move the phone somewhere else.

Someone got so annoyed by the sexy goings-on that they glued up the digits of the phone. Suspicion fell on Bob (57) when neighbours reported seeing him leaving it minutes after the phone was glued. But he was cleared by Falkirk District Court of vandalism.

1990

Barber's pole dancers

Paisley is not renowned for being in the vanguard of the permissive society. So when it was announced that Scotland's first topless barbershop was to be opened in the town it caused quite a stir among locals.

In the salon – called A Bit Off The Top – men can either choose a girl to give them a £25 haircut or a massage in a private booth. The Urban Group, the Glasgow-based company behind the venture, had recruited former lap dancers who are trained stylists to cut hair. The news provoked a furious response from church leaders and politicians. Sandra White MSP thundered, 'It's an insult to pretend it's normal for a girl to be topless while cutting hair', while a local minister branded the barbers as 'sordid'.

But one of the staff – buxom Leanne (26) – strongly defended her job. The stunning brunette, who has a huge 34D bust, said: 'We're not ashamed of our bodies and we're not doing anything wrong. A Bit Off The Top is saucy, not dirty. My attitude is: if you've got it, flaunt it.'

2004

Bald Bowie's hair-raising attacks

Leonard Bowie admitted two 'horrific offences' against vulnerable women and was jailed for eight years by Lord Wheatley at Edinburgh High Court in 2002. The judge said that Bowie's aggression towards women was related to a sexual fetish about hair, which was impossible to treat.

Depressed binge-drinker Bowie (62) had taken complete stranger Mary Mullady (51) to his Aberdeen bedsit for a drink and a haircut in August 2001 but he scalped her with a razor, leaving only a few inches of skin and scarring her for life. His blood-soaked victim was found hairless in the street by police constable Neil Montgomery. Bowie was also convicted of groping the breasts of a 59-year-old woman with Down's syndrome while he washed and cut her hair.

When police raided his room, they discovered blood, hair and a large collection of razors and scissors. Defence lawyer Frances McMenamin told the court that Bowie – who ironically is bald – had an abnormal interest in hair and admitted it regularly featured in his sexual fantasies. Police believed he was responsible for other unsolved scalping attacks on women. He had also been convicted of scalping Anne Reilly – a woman convicted of murdering her husband – in 1983 and had been imprisoned for four years for that offence.

In recognition of his services to Grampian police and the community, including securing Bowie's conviction, constable Montgomery was presented with an MBE by the Queen in July 2004.

2002

Don't try this at home

Although extremely dangerous, there are people who try to experience longer and more powerful orgasms by restricting the flow of oxygen to the brain during crucial moments – a condition called hypoxyphilia or auto-erotic asphyxia. But sometimes things go belly-up. In the loft at their Hampshire home, Lieutenant Robert Thomson (26), originally from Lanarkshire, was found by his pregnant wife Julie hanging from a beam by a strap attached to a neck collar. He was wearing a rubber mask, thigh-high PVC boots, black stockings and a leather basque.

Police officers investigating the case – similar to that of INXS rock star Michael Hutchence who also died during a bizarre sex game – found a variety of sadomasochistic sex aids in Thomson's bedroom. Julie Thomson told an inquest in Winchester that she saw something black hanging down from inside the loft and thought it was a dummy. Coroner Grahame Short concluded that Lieutenant Thomson had indulged in auto-erotic asphyxia and was a victim of his own misjudgement.

2000

Sex-mad Sheena took the biscuit

When pub landlady Sheena Brennan applied to renew her licence for the Anchor bar in Buckie, police made a series of objections. The licensing board heard that Brennan (35) was involved in kerb crawling and the owners of a local biscuit factory complained that she had pestered their young male workers for sex.

One victim, Gareth Roberts (22), was offered a lift to work at five in the morning by Brennan and her husband Billy Richardson. When they stopped for a 'toilet break', Brennan undressed and offered Roberts sex, with the prospect of a threesome when Richardson returned! Chief inspector Alan Smith told the licensing board that Roberts turned down the offer but Richardson returned to the car with his trousers around his ankles and he proceeded to have sex with Brennan, before they continued the journey.

The licensing board – which also heard that the pub was

used for late-night and underage drinking – unanimously decided that Brennan was unfit to hold a licence and the boozer was closed twenty-one days later when she failed to lodge an appeal within the time limit. It was also alleged that people had sex on pool tables in the pub and that drinkers streaked to a nearby scampi factory in a bizarre game known as the Scampi Run.

2003

Give the dog a bonk

When she got out of bed because of morning sickness, pregnant Suzanne Roberts (38) heard 'strange noises' and caught her depraved husband Darran Emms having sex with her pet Rhodesian Ridgeback dog in their porch. She immediately dumped Emms after four years of marriage, but was unable to forget what he did to the dog and reported the incident to police.

At Cupar Sheriff Court, defence lawyer John Stirling said Emms – of Kingskettle, Fife – admitted the offence and claimed it was a 'single act of frustration' because of the state of his marriage, but now both his marriage and his social life were destroyed. Sheriff George Evans admonished him because he had suffered enough already and suggested that he should undergo counselling. Suzanne Roberts was disgusted by the decision and said: 'It's totally unbelievable. He has ruined our marriage and our family life and he has never had the decency to apologise.'

2003

Randy riggers bugged porn

Red-faced Apache Corporation management tried to hide why they suddenly evacuated workers from their Delta platform in the North Sea's Forties field. The riggers were helicoptered home when an insect infestation was found in bedding and pest controllers brought in by the US oil firm identified the mysterious creatures as 'chirping book lice', which are harmless to humans but are not uncommon.

The affected cabins were sealed off to prevent the lice spreading to other parts of the platform. While rooting out the bugs, the pest control officers traced the outbreak to a huge hoard of adult magazines and the whole lot had to be removed in forty plastic bin bags. The randy riggers had apparently stashed the porn on the oil platform over a period of several years. I am surprised that the bugs managed to get into the magazines given that the pages were probably stuck together!

2003

A bloody good screw

Prisoner Marc Revie revealed how nookie-mad turnkey Fiona Buchanan seduced him while he was on remand in Barlinnie, one of Scotland's toughest prisons. Revie (22), from Paisley, had been remanded in custody in May 1999 for a vicious assault and attempted robbery on a random passer-by (a crime for which he was later convicted).

Buchanan seduced him in July 1999 following a visit to the prison doctor. After this initial encounter, he claimed he enjoyed regular romps with Buchanan while inside: she performed oral sex on him in his cell and they also had intercourse in the warder's office. But his most shocking allegation was that Buchanan masturbated herself on the landing outside his cell, while his fellow cons were all in their cells. When Revie was released in March 2000, the strange affair petered out. But news of it reached a Sunday newspaper and Buchanan resigned in disgrace in May, before having to explain herself at a disciplinary hearing.

2000

Beaver man was porn star

Parents were horrified when they discovered that scoutmaster Joe Kerr featured as 'Jessica' in a series of hardcore porn films. Kerr worked with boys aged between 5 and 8 in a beaver pack in Dalmuir, East Dunbartonshire.

Transvestite Kerr (40) liked to dress in women's underwear for bondage and flagellation scenes with women and gay men. But a former friend who saw one of the videos reported him. Scout Association bosses suspended Kerr, who looked after the boys for ninety minutes during weekly beaver-pack meetings. A spokesman said: 'We have very firm rules on what we consider to be the right sort of roles for those involved in running our movement.' Presumably porn star isn't one of them!

1998

Keeping up with the Joneses!

When Welsh songster and hunk Tom Jones announced on BBC Radio 1 that he kept his willy nice and fresh by dipping it in Listerine mouthwash, one daft fan thought he might increase his popularity with the ladies by copying him. Unfortunately, his member got well and truly stuck in the narrow-necked Listerine bottle!

Described as a thirty-something 'nerdy wee man with glasses', he turned up at Edinburgh Royal Infirmary's casualty department wearing a baggy coat but no trousers. The 'victim' showed a nurse his agonised and swollen tadger trapped in the bottle of mouthwash and explained that he tried washing it in Listerine after hearing about Jones. He had attempted to free himself from the bottle for hours, but his member just became more swollen and even more painful. Medical staff finally managed to free the hapless chap using ice and lubricant.

1999

London to Aberdeen sexpress

Passengers on the overnight London to Aberdeen coach service woke up and discovered a couple in their forties having intercourse on the bus, apparently oblivious to their neighbours. Spencer Harrison from Fraserburgh said that the half-naked woman was so consumed by passion that she lost control and kept hitting her head off the luggage rack. Other passengers saw what was going on but didn't alert the driver. Mr Harrison attempted to ignore the randy pair's activities and tried to get to sleep. Later, the couple mentioned their antics to nearby passengers, saying: 'We hope you weren't watching us.' Spencer Harrison said: 'I certainly wasn't. The woman was pretty ugly.'

1991

Watt next for cone man?

Ross Watt (34), whose previous convictions included simulating sex with a training shoe in a public place, was arrested and charged when he encouraged a group of teenagers to watch him in action with a traffic cone at the foot of Edinburgh's Calton Hill!

Watt had approached teenage drivers asking to buy their trainers (so he could have sex with the shoes) but they all refused. He then offered them a public show with the nearest available object, an orange-and-white traffic cone. The motorists circled their cars around the oddball, encouraging him with shouts of 'give it some'. He rolled about on the ground rubbing his genitals against the cone for nearly twenty minutes. Police arrived and promptly arrested him.

When he committed the offence, Watt was receiving psychiatric treatment at the Royal Edinburgh hospital and was on probation for whacking his groin with a training shoe while standing next to a window in his Edinburgh flat. Watt had a ten-year history of similarly outrageous offences.

At Edinburgh Sheriff Court, Sheriff Mhairi Stephen was told that Watt had an extensive support network paid from the public purse to tackle his persistent offending. Defence lawyer Andy Gilbertson bizarrely compared Watt's performance to 'a piece of Edinburgh Fringe street theatre', adding that many people 'were probably disappointed there was not a repeat performance during the festival'. However, Watt's disgusting behaviour distressed some witnesses. Sheriff Stephen took the view that Watt had committed a breach of the piece and admonished him.

2002–2003

Well covered

Czech-born blonde beauty Petra Morgan (24), whose boobs have been surgically enlarged from a bouncy 32C to a whopping 32EE, wobbled into the *Guinness Book of Records* with the world's most expensive body part after insuring her assets for £10 million! The cash will be handed out if 'entirely due to circumstances beyond the control of the insured, the insured breast(s) become damaged to such an extent that the insured is prevented from continuing in her career as a model'.

Petra stars in naughty porn movies – mainly for Canadian and German punters – and lived in East Dunbartonshire's Milngavie with a Scottish boyfriend from 1998. Petra's film company 'Lovely Girls', whose annual profits hit £50 million, paid the £56,500 annual premium. Manager Dickie Longfellow said 'Breasts are big business these days and Petra's our top model who makes us most money', while Simon Burgess, the managing partner of London-based insurers Goodfellows, described the mammary deal as 'a wonderful and uplifting experience'.

2001

4

Love and marriage

As the song goes, marriage is 'an institute you can't disparage' . . . although many have tried.

The treachery of Kinky Knickers

Alec Smith was head-over-heels in love with bride-to-be, Agnes Hailes. He met her through their mutual interest in CB radio and Alec had quickly become devoted to the girl with the call-sign of Kinky Knickers. He scrimped and saved for months to pay for a glittering wedding. Such was his devotion that the 22-year-old storeman cycled the twenty miles to and from his work to save on bus fares. When the big day arrived no expense was spared. There were seven bridesmaids, three flower girls and three page boys. The wedding cars were Mercedes and a video company would record the joy of Alec and Agnes and their 230 guests. All in all, the bill for their nuptials in Cambuslang came to £3,500.

But it all went horribly wrong on their first night as husband and wife. As they lay in bed – with Alec no doubt looking for a reward for all his hard work – Agnes (24) dropped a bombshell. She told him to keep his hands to himself and stay on the far side of the bed. At first he thought it was wedding-night nerves and eventually drifted off to sleep. But when he woke up the next morning he discovered her second bombshell. She had slipped out of bed during the night and left him forever. The marriage had lasted all of twelve hours.

Then the truth came out. She claimed that she had never loved him and had only gone through with the wedding to keep a promise she had made to her father as he lay on his deathbed. Her father had liked and respected Alec, so much so that he made Agnes promise to marry him. But she had soon changed her mind about marrying him and blamed her family for pressuring her into tying the knot with a man she did not love. Nevertheless, Alec was understandably bitter: 'I want an annulment or divorce. We never made love.'

Other strands in the story were equally bizarre. It transpired that Agnes had not taken a spur of the moment decision on that fateful first night. She had in fact told the bridesmaids of her plan to leave Alec immediately after they were married but sworn them to secrecy. She also confessed that she had been seeing another man for seven weeks before the wedding. And then there was her explanation of how she how she got the CB nickname of Kinky Knickers: 'I love wearing exotic underwear.' In the aftermath of the wedding, Agnes was now living with a married couple, Willie and Angela Brown. She vehemently denied having an affair with Willie but admitted having talked for hours on end to him in a sexy way on the CB.

But there was a happy ending for the noble Alec. Two months after the wedding he met the new love of his life, June Brown. Despite the fact that Agnes had publicly asked him to take her back he was determined to start a new life: 'There is only one girl I care for now and that is June. All I want to do is forget my wife.'

1988

Randy meat-man Willie porked best pal's wife

It would come as a shock to any husband. To wake up and find your best pal having hot sex with your wife. But that is what happened to a Johnstone man after he invited colleague and friend Willie Craig (33) to stay overnight.

This version of the eternal triangle all started when slaughterman Craig arrived at the house of his buddy and his wife armed with a bottle of vodka and cans of lager. After the trio had enjoyed a wee swally they decided to retire for the evening. While the husband and wife went up to bed Willie slept on the couch in the front room. But nature called and the visitor had to use the bathroom, which was upstairs. As he was about to go back downstairs his hostess called out to him: 'Is that you chief?'

Intrigued, he looked into the bedroom and saw the woman lying on top of the bed beside her sleeping husband. She was wearing only a T-shirt and panties. There was a cigarette in her hand and a glass of vodka on the bedside table. Willie sat down next to her and soon they were kissing and cuddling. Nature took its course and before long they were having passionate sex. But they must have disturbed the sleeping husband who woke up ten minutes into their lovemaking. As Willie desperately scrambled to pull on his trousers, his pal shouted, 'What the hell do youse two think you're doing?'

But worse was to follow for Craig. The woman reported him for sexual assault while she was sleeping. During his trial at Glasgow High Court she claimed that she hadn't woken up during the sex because she had taken sleeping pills and a lot of drink. Craig was asked if he wasn't concerned that the woman's husband was asleep in the bed only a few inches away and replied. 'No. I had other things on my mind.'

The jury returned a verdict of not proven and the accused walked into the arms of his loving wife, Cathy, who had forgiven him. The trial judge, Lord McCluskey summed it up perfectly: 'We get some bizarre glimpses of life in the High Court and this was certainly one of them.'

1991

He didn't know bride was on the game

Ian McAdam, a salesman from Hamilton, was stunned when he found out his wife of just ten days was a prostitute who also starred in porn films. He first met Italian-born Marina de Sanctis three years before and she told him she worked for a women's underwear firm. But one day he went to the address in Glasgow's Holland Street and found that it was in reality an establishment called Tropical Palms, a seedy sauna. He found Marina – who worked under the name of Alana – waiting for clients. 'I was boiling mad. I screamed, "What are you doing here?" and she screamed exactly the same thing to me. . . . I couldn't believe it. This was the girl I married, a common hooker treating me like one of her customers.'

But Marina was not finished yet. She reported Ian for unpaid traffic fines and, while he was temporarily in police custody, ransacked their flat in Hamilton and stole his clothes, car keys and driving licence. She left a note signed, 'The whore you married.'

Ian explained he married Marina after she told him she was pregnant and claims that only a few days after the wedding she told him she had an abortion. He insisted that he could never forgive her and had consulted a lawyer about a divorce.

1997

Man-mad Mary must have matrimony

Some women will go to any lengths to get a husband. But few are as dedicated, or as methodical, as Mary Wilkinson of Dumfries. Only three weeks after the death of her third husband in January 1992, the 68-year-old was advertising in the local paper for a new man.

If anyone knew how to play the lonely heart it was Mary. She found her first husband, Fred King, a Dumfries widower, through an advert in her local paper in Duns. Fred was one of seventy men who replied. Then, when he died in 1975, James Kay, also a widower, was the lucky respondent from the fifty hopefuls who were captivated by another newspaper ad.

Sadly, James passed away in 1979. Mary may have been losing her touch as only six men wrote to her following yet another advert. But she still managed to find a kindred spirit in bachelor Grant Wilkinson and the happy couple tied the knot in 1980.

Mary is unabashed about her motives: 'I just can't live on my own. I get lonely and need companionship.' And as for her ideal man, 'Someone kind and respectable just like the others.'

1992

In the worst possible taste

Scotland's tackiest-ever wedding was held at Gretna's famous registry office. Steve Howarth, the grossly overweight groom, was dressed in a teacher's gown, complete with mortarboard and cane. And his 16-year-old bride, Tessa Gunton – who sported braces on her teeth – dressed as a St Trinian's-style schoolgirl showing six inches of bare thigh, along with mini-skirt, stockings and suspenders.

The odd couple, from Thornton in Lancashire, met when Tessa was at school in nearby Fleetwood. Howarth had been married twice before and his 14-year-old son James was at the wacky ceremony. The groom denied he had cradle-snatched a child bride from his son and claimed that he and Gunton were not worried about the age difference as 'they loved each other'. Gunton said it was her idea to have a 'romantic' wedding in Gretna, and to dress up in school outfits. The delightful pair gestured rudely to onlookers as they left the registry office.

Following the wedding photographs, the couple headed to the blacksmith's at Gretna Green for the traditional blessing over the anvil – and the groom gave his bride a cheeky smack on her bottom with his cane.

2000

Assault with a deadly shampoo

Former soldier Colin Slane (28) was jailed for fourteen months when he was found guilty of an extraordinary assault following a six-day trial at Dundee Sheriff Court. When arrested, Slane, who knew about his ex-wife's severe allergies, allegedly told police he smeared Silvikrin shampoo on the door handle of her Dundee home to 'get her back', although he was prohibited from going within 100 yards of her house following an earlier attack. Heather Brown (33) was left gasping for breath and ended up in hospital after she touched the door handle.

However, in court, Slane denied endangering Heather's life with the shampoo in January 1999, and he also denied spitting in her face and damaging her car by jumping on the roof and bonnet in August 1998. The jury was told that Heather could suffer a potentially fatal anaphylactic shock if she came into contact with a wide range of everyday items.

In fact, due to her health problems, Sheriff Richard Davidson, court officials, lawyers and jurors agreed not to eat peanuts or use perfume, deodorants or other toiletries during the case, while journalists and members of the public were ordered to leave if they had been in contact with the 'dangerous' substances. These safety measures were said to be unprecedented in a Scottish court. Slane also caused a ninety-minute delay when he was removed from the court to have gel washed from his hair.

2000

Hubby became her dad

In a remarkable turn of events, dumped wife Alison Smith performed her duties as bridesmaid – while her 44-year-old mother Pat married Alison's ex-husband George Greenhowe (21) on her twentieth birthday.

Alison had let her mum move into the marital home in

Arbroath when Pat walked out on her dad, Allan. But, only ten days after Alison and George's wedding in November 2001, she caught Pat and George in bed together. Alison divorced George for adultery, naming her mum as the other woman.

When Pat and George's wedding was announced all hell broke loose. Allan described the outrageous pair as 'sick', Pat's mum Patricia Williamson disowned her daughter and George's mother Ann said she wouldn't attend. However, Scots law says that a man cannot marry his ex-wife's mother if his former wife is still alive, and officials from Arbroath's registry office warned the couple their plans were illegal.

But Alison, who had forgiven George since their divorce, still got him as a step-dad following a bizarre humanist ceremony (which isn't legally recognised) at the Cliffburn hotel in Arbroath in September 2003. At the event – organised by lifestyle magazine *Closer* – Pat and George were 'married' by a 'minister' who was formerly an undertaker.

The couple's standards were highlighted when, instead of knickers, Pat wore a musical thong that played 'Here Comes The Bride' as they exchanged vows. The newlyweds then announced their wish to have a baby, using George's cousin Christine as a surrogate mother if necessary. The reception broke up in chaos when members of George's family got involved in a drunken brawl. The police swooped on the hotel, George's brother and uncle spent the night in police cells and a man and two teenage boys were charged with breach of the peace and police assault.

Alison, who had fainted during the reception, revealed a tattoo on her arm which read 'I love dad', presumably referring to George! She obviously had not learned much from her first experience of marriage because, while eight months pregnant, she was dumped by text message four days before her next wedding when fiancé Peter Knight got cold feet.

Amazingly, the ceremony went ahead almost as planned in February 2004 when Alison's ex-boyfriend Daniel Innes (18) volunteered to take Peter's place. It took just forty-eight hours for Alison to agree to marry unemployed Daniel but she didn't know who the father of her child was: it could have been Peter, Daniel or his brother John. She said that she loved Daniel because he 'made her laugh, he is good looking and he makes her feel secure'. But maybe it was all for the benefit of *Closer* magazine, which was the first to report the latest development in the marriage-go-round.

2003–2004

He married her anyway

At the Co-operative funeral parlour in Musselburgh, Michael Allen married his fiancée Rebecca Dickson, a week after her death! The unfortunate pair had celebrated their engagement with bootleg vodka contaminated by a high proportion of methanol and it had killed poor Rebecca.

A priest conducted the ceremony and blessed the union while Rebecca (42) lay in her open coffin and Michael (52) placed a wedding ring on the deceased woman's finger. Four days after the strange ceremony, Rebecca was laid to rest at Tranent cemetery. I don't know if the marriage was legally binding but I certainly hope that it wasn't consummated.

2003

'Throw her in the Clyde'

Donald Cooper should have been distraught. June, his wife of thirty-five years, had died in hospital. She had been devoted to him and attended to his every need.

But Cooper (59) declined to make funeral arrangements for her. He said, 'I couldn't care if they threw her in the Clyde.' He even refused to go to the funeral and the only mourners were the gravediggers and a couple of pallbearers. June was buried in an unmarked, pauper's grave. Revd Hamish McIntosh, who carried out the ceremony, said 'It was tragic, heartless.'

The Coopers, from Leicestershire, had been on holiday in Scotland when June (58) broke her ankle and went into hospital for an operation. Salesman Cooper left her there and went back to England to collect his new car. A neighbour said that he spent two days washing the vehicle before the hospital rang to say she had died of complications related to the op. Cooper signed a death certificate on the day of her demise but would not get involved in organising the funeral. He also refused to pay anything towards the cost.

Cooper later claimed he couldn't afford to pay for the funeral expenses because his wife had left debts of £20,000, a claim that was later disproved.

1997

Horror in room 508

Staff in holiday hotels are used to the unedifying behaviour of tourists and very little surprises them. But hotel manager Felipe Martinez and his staff were genuinely shocked when they saw the inside of room 508 in their hotel in San Antonio, Ibiza. It was occupied by a couple from Loanhead in Midlothian and their 3-year-old son.

When a chambermaid entered the room – which had had a do-not-disturb sign on the door handle for a week – she found the toddler dirty and naked. He was eating from a tub of margarine. His parents were lying drunk out of their minds on the bed surrounded by twenty empty liquor bottles. The room was in such a disgusting state that it later had to be completely redecorated and all the furniture was destroyed.

It was discovered that the boy had lived on crisps and margarine for a week and had had not been bathed during that time. Hotel staff were in tears over his predicament. A decision was taken to fly him home without his parents because they were too drunk to look after him. The confused tot slept for most of the flight and was collected by his grandparents when he got home.

Senor Martinez was plainly bemused and said: 'I have never seen anything like this in sixteen years in this job. We were met by an appalling sight. Both these people were drunk and the room was in a disgusting state.' As for the boy's parents, they admitted they had a drink problem. In Scotland, social workers became involved and were considering what to do with the boy.

1995

5

Same shit, different day

The wage slaves of Scotland are fed up. And with working conditions like these it's little wonder.

You diddies

Busty Charlotte McDonald was told to cover up her crown jewels while working at Edinburgh Castle. While men queued up to be photographed with her, some women visitors were unhappy about how much of her huge 36 EE boobs she was revealing.

Charlotte (25) wore a low-cut costume while selling guide books at the castle. Her bosses, Historic Scotland, said they had received a written complaint and told her to cover up by wearing a scarf over the top of her dress.

The buxom beauty was indignant: 'It's a storm in an E cup. I am proud of my body. I normally wear tight-fitting clothes so I am used to men staring.'

She was sacked by Historic Scotland but later got her first break in showbiz when she was picked to play a sexy showgirl in a production of *The Barber of Seville* at the Cottier theatre, Glasgow.

1996

Charlotte McDonald

Number one or two?

Ductform Ventilation of Glenrothes infuriated staff when signs were pinned to toilet doors telling workers to write down how long they had spent answering calls of nature. They were also asked to describe what they did in there by marking P or S on a form.

Production manager Edward Brown defended the decision and said he was only trying to assess how much work he could get out of his men in a week. Eddie, you got it all wrong. It is the God-given right of Scottish workers to shite in the work's time and not in their own.

1997

Do it yourself

Workers at a new B & Q store in East Kilbride were horrified when managers asked them to greet each other with lines from the Muppets song. Instead of 'good morning', staff were expected to sing 'mahna mahna' to their colleagues who would respond with the song's chorus which goes, 'doo doo be-doo-doo'.

The crazy idea, designed to boost morale, was thought up during a managers' brainstorming session at the B & Q 'university' – a learning centre in Cambuslang, near Glasgow. Managers were so excited about the idea that they spent most of the training day running about singing the song.

But their staff were not impressed. Some threatened to quit, while others refused to transfer to the East Kilbride store. As one said, 'There is no way I will be joining in . . . if people talk to me like this I'll be more likely to tell them to piss off.'

2004

He disnae care

Jolly coach driver Donnie MacDonald encouraged passengers on his Shearings tour bus to find out the name of the local quack in Mallaig, Inverness-shire. The medic's name was Dr Donald Duck. He got the name before the creation of the Disney character.

But passengers invariably asked Mallaig's only traffic warden, Cathy Grant, for the answer. She got fed up and complained to her police bosses who in turn complained to Shearings. Donnie clearly thought Cathy was quackers: 'I couldn't believe it when my boss told me he'd had a complaint from the police about me. The warden claimed she couldn't get on with her duties because of me and my silly questions. Now I tell my passengers to ask anybody except her.'

As for the good doctor, he said he had learned to live with his name. He even introduced himself to the harbourmaster thus: 'Hello, I'm Donald Duck, the local quack.'

1992

Peggy hosed his hose

Nurse Peggy Botha took drastic action to stop an elderly stroke victim who was performing a sex act in the bath – by spraying him with cold water. She had been called to the scene by three of her colleagues who were bathing the man when he started playing with himself. Even when he was hoisted onto a special chair he carried on regardless, despite requests from the staff to stop. It was at this point that Nurse Botha tried to cool his ardour by turning the shower on him.

But Botha was sacked for gross misconduct by the BUPA Pentland Hill Nursing Home and she later lost her claim for unfair dismissal. The tribunal heard that loss of sexual inhibition was a possible side-effect of a stroke and ruled in favour of her employer.

2003

Hard to swallow

Guests at Glasgow's luxurious Hilton hotel were given a veritable feast with all the trimmings for their £49.95 per head Christmas dinner. A choice of succulent starters, followed by turkey, beef or salmon and finished off with a rich Christmas pudding. There were crackers too and Santa handed out presents for the kids.

But the five-star hotel was not quite as generous to its staff who were served up . . . Pot Noodle and Cup-A-Soup. To add insult to injury, workers said they had to eat the snacks lukewarm when a plumbing problem meant there was no hot water. One disgruntled member of staff said, 'It was a real case of *Upstairs Downstairs* and we thought it was a joke. It's scandalous that a company the size of Hilton treats the staff like this.'

2003

Sweet turned sour

Vicki McIntyre and Sharron McConville were sacked by Woolworth's in Dundee for stealing a sweet each. The sweets, worth only 2p, had fallen on the floor and were to be thrown in the bin. They were a Mr Blobby jelly and a fizzy-cola chew, both from the pick 'n' mix section.

The women were spotted eating the sweets by a security guard who reported them to the manager, David Duncan. He later said: 'I had to sack them. They were in a position of trust. And I could never have trusted them again after that.' His boss, area manager Terry Kelly, agreed: 'It starts with one sweet then goes on to a handful and before you know it they are stealing CDs.'

The two women took Woolworth's to an industrial tribunal. Following an initial adjourned hearing, Woolworth's backed down and agreed to give the girls a cash payoff.

1997

Stop your nagging, woman

Ivie Clelland of Motherwell was fired after he threw a cup of tea over his ex-girlfriend. Although he and Margaret Calderwood had broken up, they worked in the same factory in the town. One day she visited the area that Ivie worked in and was abusive to him. The nagging continued at tea break despite him reporting Margaret to management.

All of this may have been hard for colleagues to understand because Margaret had nagged him in sign language! They were both deaf and dumb and were employed by the Remploy factory.

An industrial tribunal ruled that Ivie's sacking was unfair because management had not investigated the incident properly. But they refused to order Remploy to give him his job back because they reasoned he was two-thirds to blame.

1991

He dropped a bombshell

A forestry worker found an unexploded world war two artillery shell, and delivered it to the foreman in a council office next to the

Eshiels gasworks, near Peebles. The tree-planter found the rusty relic when he tripped over it but, instead of making a beeline for the horizon, the man took it to council foreman John Wilson.

Mr Wilson revealed that the unnamed man found the shell lying behind the council shed and had jauntily told him: 'I think you've got a problem – but don't worry, it's not ticking.' The petrified foreman immediately contacted the police: the area was cordoned off, nearby cottages were evacuated and the bomb squad carried out a controlled explosion to disable the device.

1999

Express flitting

Bus driver Raymond Gillespie abandoned his passengers for four evenings one week while he transported furniture from his old house to a new pad in his bus. Stranded passengers angrily complained to First Glasgow and demanded to know why the X4/X5 Glasgow to Cumbernauld express hadn't turned up, so managers sent out bus inspector Brian Anderson to trace the missing vehicle.

Anderson drove to-and-fro along the service's scheduled route on the M80 and almost ran out of petrol during the search. Eventually, he spotted the bus near Cumbernauld and was amazed to see 34-year-old Gillespie heading for his Cumbernauld home instead of following the scheduled route. Anderson kept watch and followed Gillespie to his new home at Bargeddie in Glasgow, without a passenger in sight.

When the bus stopped, the inspector was astonished to find that the bus had been converted into a removal van and was filled with furniture and household goods. Gillespie's bosses at the Cumbernauld depot sacked him when they were given details of the incident. The driver's former colleagues were amazed that he thought he would get away with his bizarre flitting but they all had a good laugh at his expense.

2000

6

NHS: National Homicide Service

When the NHS found that not enough patients were being killed off by long waiting lists, it invented a new weapon of mass destruction: the MRSA superbug. And if that isn't enough, it always has the incompetence of some of its staff to fall back on.

Randy nurse bonked cancer patient

Leukaemia victim Nicky McArthur was at his lowest ebb after chemotherapy and radiation treatment for the deadly blood cancer. He had lost all his hair and felt terrible. So it was a great boost to his morale when a nurse, Norma Speirs, got the hots for him. The busty blonde was in and out of Nicky's room and even wrote him love notes. He said: 'It seemed as if no one would give me a second look . . . but she made me feel good about myself.'

The couple would later deny having sex in the hospital, but their affair took off a week before Nicky (27) was due to leave Gartnavel hospital. Forty-year-old Norma sent a note asking him to meet at Woolworths and the odd couple then had a series of steamy romps. But Nicky realised the relationship wouldn't work: Norma already had a partner, as well as two children, and 'he didn't want to be responsible for breaking up anyone's family.' And anyway, Nicky was now engaged to someone else.

Norma's colleagues were shocked, and one said: 'Norma was always a bit flirty with the men. She loved to get dolled-up for nights out and she liked a good time – but we would never have expected her to get involved with a patient. No nurse should start behaving like that with a patient.'

2004

Dr Death goes back to work

The risk of catching a superbug and croaking is often more worrying for patients than the illnesses they went into hospital for in the first place. So for a Dundee hospital to give a doctor his job back eight months after he was convicted of killing a patient is surreal.

In May 2003, at Winchester Crown Court, Dr Rajeev Srivastava was charged with manslaughter caused by gross negligence, along with his colleague, Dr Amit Misra. They had been treating Sean Phillips, a 31-year-old father-of-one, when he fell ill with toxic-shock syndrome. But they failed to take the action that could have saved his life and were too proud to ask for help. Mr Phillips, who had only gone into Southampton general hospital for routine knee-surgery, was eventually rushed into intensive care but it was too late to save his life. The jury found the mixed-up medics guilty and they were sentenced to eighteen months in prison. However, because the judge took the view that their careers had been ruined by the scandal he suspended the sentences for two years, meaning that they walked free from court.

Amazingly, the General Medical Council did not strike off either doctor and, two months after the trial, actually upgraded Srivastava's registration. By early January 2004, while only halfway through his sentence, he was back working at Ninewells hospital as a trainee registrar. His erstwhile partner-in-crime, Dr Misra also had a new job . . . as a trainee surgeon in Newcastle. Both hospitals were quick to reassure the public that no patients were at risk!

Quite understandably, Mr Phillips's family were incensed and his partner Annabel Grant said: 'It is completely sickening. My son has to have counselling for what he's gone through. In his own little world he's been expecting his dad to come home every day.'

2004

Can I get you an application form for EXIT?

Not content with employing a killer as a surgeon, Ninewells hospital asked patients if they had ever thought of suicide (faced with the prospect of treatment in Ninewells, they probably had). Alex McCallum (63), who has Parkinson's disease, was given a questionnaire on which the last question was 'Have you thought of the possibility that you might make away with yourself?'

As his wife Frances said, 'What sort of a question is that to ask someone who is ill? You don't know what it could do to them.' The feeble excuse given by Ninewells was that it was trying to identify patients with treatable depression.

1995

Thick as two short planks

The bedside manner of Dr Richard Makower of Glasgow's Royal Infirmary left a lot to be desired when a patient with a serious spinal injury was wheeled into casualty. Gordon McCann (44) had been assaulted by a thug with a plank of wood and had suffered a spinal injury that paralysed him from the neck down. This cut no ice with Makower, who made the following pronouncements:

- That Mr McCann was a 'drunken nutter'.
- After lifting up Gordon's arm and dropping it, he said 'It's the funniest quadriplegic I've ever seen.'
- As Mr McCann fell to the floor after being lifted up, Makower said, 'If he doesn't move in half an hour get him removed by the police.'

As Gordon McCann quite literally could not move, two bobbies arrived and took him away. They drove him to a spot ten miles from the hospital and, astonishingly, dumped him on a grass verge.

Makower was later found guilty of serious professional

misconduct by the General Medical Council, which also described him as callous. But, in the best traditions of the NHS, he was later promoted to senior registrar at a hospital in Kent. The two cops were disciplined and fined.

1992

Tears of a cabbie

Shocked passengers using Shervill's taxis of Airdrie couldn't believe their ears when they heard a request on the radio to pick up a dead baby from a mortuary.

The baby had died after a full-term pregnancy and its body was to be taken back to Bellshill maternity hospital after a post mortem at Yorkhill hospital in Glasgow. For a fare of £11 the cabbie put the body in the front seat of his taxi and drove the 16 miles to Bellshill. He found the experience harrowing in the extreme: 'I feel absolutely terrible. When I got home to my house afterwards I just burst into tears. That wee baby deserved something a bit more dignified than being put in a taxi.'

1991

Hospital from hell

Glasgow's Victoria Infirmary became notorious in the mid-1990s for its inefficiency and callous disregard for patients. The treatment of patients in its geriatric ward is a case in point. An inquiry by management revealed:

- Hundreds of pounds belonging to patients had gone missing.
- A Jew was taunted about concentration camps and gold fillings.
- A vegetarian patient was sick after being given meat to eat.
- A Catholic was refused the last rites, while Catholic staff were called 'Fenians, papes and tims'.

- Disturbed patients were called frailies and one was slapped in the face with a wet cloth.
- When a male nurse was asked to help with a patient struggling for breath he said, 'Tell me when she is dead.'

Unusually for the NHS the abuse in the geriatric ward was not swept under the carpet and a number of staff were suspended or sacked.

1996

Mum saw aborted foetus in jar

Following a painful abortion at Glasgow's Stobhill hospital, Nicola McManus was directed into a room by hospital staff so she could answer a call from her anxious husband – but she was horrified to see her nine-week-old foetus in a clearly labelled jar on a shelf.

The 27-year-old mother of three from Lennoxtown was given the RU486 abortion pill, which does not require surgery and is supposed to make abortions easier by causing a miscarriage. However, she claimed the procedure wasn't discussed with her beforehand and that she was in pain for hours. She also said that hospital staff made her feel 'just like a number'.

Although an apology was given by North Glasgow NHS Trust, Ms McManus was still angry about the outrageous error. She was told that patients don't normally have access to the room where she saw the jar with its grisly contents. She got her apology (of sorts) in a letter from the trust's general manager, Mary McGinley: 'Unfortunately, the products of conception from your termination were in a labelled jar ready to be sent to pathology and awaiting collection. The ward sister apologises for the obvious distress this has caused you.'

2002

They wanted sex but not their leg over

Consultant surgeon Robert Smith believed that amputating a patient's healthy leg was the most satisfying operation of his career! Mr Smith, of Falkirk and District Royal Infirmary, justified his actions by arguing it was better he did the job properly than leave disturbed patients to attempt it themselves.

Patients with body dismorphic disorder believe they have imperfections and will go to any lengths to amputate healthy limbs. In some cases sufferers have shot the limbs off, or even had them chopped off by trains. The related sex fetish apotemnophilia – estimated to affect only two hundred people worldwide – leads sufferers to crave contact with amputees or to have amputations for their own sexual gratification.

Unsurprisingly, surgeons around the world refuse to carry out such amputations, but news of Mr Smith's 'pioneering' work spread on the internet and he had a waiting list of six when his NHS trust found out and demanded a halt to the ops, which had originally been approved by trust executives. Mr Smith was disappointed with the decision and claimed that he would never carry out an amputation on a patient who was only seeking sexual arousal.

A few days after the story came to light, it was revealed that Kevin Wright from Colchester had had his healthy lower leg amputated by Mr Smith at Falkirk Royal in 1997. Mr Wright had been assessed by two psychiatrists who concluded he did not want the op for sexual reasons. Mr Smith agreed, although he knew Mr Wright ran OverGround, a fetish website featuring amputees and people sexually excited by them. Mr Wright said he felt he had an alien 'extra limb' and that the operation had made him 'complete'. He paid around £2,500 for the use of NHS facilities although Mr Smith did not charge a fee.

2000

Bungling docs missed melon-sized tumour for eleven years

When Christine MacCallum developed a tumour that weighed a stone, mixed-up medics told her to go on a diet. For eleven years doctors told her she was overweight and distended after childbirth despite the fact that the massive melon-sized growth was only on one side of her body. As she explained: 'The lump used to hang on one side from the front of my leg right round to the back.' She kept asking doctors why the 'fat' was only on one side of her body but it was never investigated.

Christine also had a tumour the size of a tennis ball on her leg and it was so big that it often caused embarrassment when she was out: 'Young children would point at it' she explained, 'and one time I was in a shopping centre and noticed the security guard was looking at me. I think he thought I had stolen something because I had the massive lump on my leg.'

The 42-year-old, from Alexandria in Dunbartonshire, had to suffer the condition until her daughter Sarah was found to have a tumour on her neck. Then doctors realised their mistake and diagnosed mother and daughter with neurofibromatosis, a rare genetic condition that causes benign tumour-like lumps to grow anywhere on the body. The NF tumours can be life-threatening as they sometimes lead to high blood pressure, spinal defects and many other problems. It was particularly devastating for Christine as she had just successfully battled breast cancer.

After undergoing a four-and-a-half hour operation to remove the tumour Christine MacCallum was on the road to recovery and determined to live life to the full, despite the realisation that the tumour could come back.

2004

Off their trolley

Ninewells hospital called Karen Wilson when her father David, who was being treated for deep-vein thrombosis, took a turn for the worse. When Ms Wilson and her mother arrived at the hospital, they found his body lying on an unattended trolley in a corridor – before being informed he was dead.

The grieving women sent a letter of complaint to Ninewells but were told that staff on duty denied the body was Mr Wilson's and, in consequence, there would be no investigation. It seems unlikely that the women would incorrectly identify such a close relative!

2001

Bleeping nuisance

An ex-nurse at Ninewells hospital alleged that staff turned off the sound on vital heart monitors because the high-pitched sounds were annoying. Terminally ill patients had to suffer in silence, while some had even died and remained undiscovered for over an hour. It was also claimed that visitors turned up and found their relatives dead in bed while the nurses were busy elsewhere.

2001

Not such little angels

Following closure of the last wards at Belvidere hospital in Glasgow the building and its grounds were pillaged by nurses and thousands of pounds worth of NHS property was stolen. Duvet covers were stripped from beds, garden furniture disappeared, apple and pear trees vanished from the garden and pictures and mirrors were pinched. It was even said that a low-loader was brought in by one nurse's husband to assist with the removal of bulky stolen goods!

Although some staff volunteered to return stolen goods, the health board informed the police.

1998

Dr Do-Little

A Scottish hospital consultant was off work for nearly five years on her full salary of £70,000 a year. Dr Pamela Stephen (later Harper) was suspended in December 1995 after colleagues at Perth Royal Infirmary accused her of serious professional misconduct.

In July 1998, several senior politicians, including Scottish Office health minister and former brain surgeon Sam Galbraith, condemned the delays and the consequent waste of public money. Dr Harper – by then nicknamed Dr Do-Little by the press – admitted that the case was a terrible waste of both healthcare money and her skills as a geriatrician but said that 'some of the working relationships were not ideal' at the hospital.

Although her suspension was lifted following a government inquiry led by an eminent physician, she remained at home for two more years considering an offer of re-employment. Tayside University Hospitals NHS Trust eventually lost patience and decided that Dr Harper's refusal to accept their offer left 'no option but to terminate her employment'. She was finally sacked in November 2000.

The dispute, which cost taxpayers a staggering £350,000, began when Dr Harper fell out with her kilt-wearing colleague, Dr Ian Lightbody. They had worked together successfully for eleven years before a catastrophic 'clash of personalities'.

1995–2000

7

Barmy social workers and our holiday-camp prisons

We all know the criminal justice system is run for the benefit of thugs, thieves and junkies. And it's getting worse every day.

Has been's fear-and-love loops

Given all the scandals their 'profession' had been responsible for, the Scottish Executive thought social workers needed a morale booster. So it paid washed-up pop star Pat Kane's firm £50,000 to write a brochure called *Re-Imagining Social Work*. The barmy brochure produced by the self-styled 'cultural consultant' said that re-imagining social work is built on four core ideas:

- Consciousness
- Fear-and-love loops
- Play ethic
- Four quadrants

His fear-and-love loops, the brochure points out, 'move us away from the inner realms towards a contemplation of knowledge beyond the self. They describe two dominant ways that we choose to know the world – through control (the Fear Loop), and through participation (the Love Loop).'

A number of Scottish councils also sent staff to lectures given by the former Hue and Cry singer at £440 a head. South Lanarkshire Council spent £10,000, while Edinburgh City Council sent twenty staff to a course in the city's luxurious Malmaison hotel. The course asked social workers to examine depictions of their job in Hollywood movies such as *The Cell* starring Jennifer Lopez, and *Lilo and Stitch.*

Right on, Pat.

2004

Taxi for junkie

Loony social work bosses at West Dunbartonshire Council used taxpayers' money to pay for taxis to take homeless drug addicts to collect their methadone fixes. The trips cost up to £64 a time.

The pampered junkies were driven from Glasgow to pharmacies up to twenty miles away to get the heroin substitute from their home towns of Dumbarton and Alexandria. One junkie was taken four times in a single week to a pharmacy in Alexandria from his hostel in the south side of Glasgow.

The council said that only certain pharmacies could prescribe methadone with each handling a set number of addicts; when their quota was full they had to refer people to pharmacies outside the area they currently lived in. But a spokeswoman refused to say why the junkies could not have been given bus passes or told to make their own way.

2004

They recommended community service . . . for a murderer

Thomas Shields is one of Scotland's most savage killers. A brutal, merciless thug responsible for a crime so violent it sends a shiver down the spine. He was just 15 when he murdered a total stranger in an unprovoked attack in Garthamlock, Glasgow in 2003. Andrew Herd (27) was speaking to two women at a bus stop when Shields ran across the road and hit him on the head with a heavy metal pole. The teenage thug, out of his head on vodka, continued to hit the defenceless man with the pole before throwing it into the middle of the road and walking away.

But he was not finished yet. Shields returned to the scene and began to jump up and down on his victim's head as if it was a trampoline. A passing bus driver thought Shields was jumping on a pile of rubbish but was horrified to discover it was actually a man's head.

Despite the clear evidence against him Shields pleaded not guilty, but was nevertheless convicted of murder at the High Court in Edinburgh. Given the level of brutality involved the judge, Lord Hardie, was staggered when he read the pre-sentence report by Glasgow City Council's social work department. He said that the report considered the possibility of a fine, community service and probation. A social worker had even spoken to Shields to see if he would be willing to accept such a sentence.

But no-nonsense beak Lord Hardie was having none of it. He castigated the social workers involved for their 'absurd' report which he said was 'a total waste of public money'. He jailed Shields for life with a recommendation that he should serve at least eighteen years before being considered for release.

2004

'All over me like a rash'

Social workers are trained to empathise with their unfortunate clients, to be a shoulder to cry on, a friendly face in an often harsh world. But Vicki McIntosh (24) perhaps took this a little too far when it came to Billy, a 15-year-old boy in her care. She drove him to the countryside and had sex with him when he was spaced out on drugs she had bought.

As Billy explained: 'She started to touch me then we had sex in the car. She was all over me like a rash. She told me she loved me, that I was special and this was our secret.'

McIntosh first met Billy, a strapping six-footer, at a child unit in Falkirk where workers tried to get close to the children and create a family atmosphere. But it was clear from the beginning that she was taking this too far in Billy's case. As one of her colleagues said, 'She singled the boy out in the classic abuser pattern. She put him on a pedestal. And told him he was special. Then she took advantage of him.'

Their affair went on for months and only came to light when one of the other children in the unit broke down and told another worker about it. Despite the fact that McIntosh was transferred to another job, she kept turning up near Billy and even wrote a thirty-page letter to his mum declaring her love for him.

Later, in court, McIntosh admitted two charges of shameless and indecent conduct and was jailed for nine months. She was also put on the register of sex offenders for ten years. In her defence she said, 'I'm no cradle snatcher. This is all wrong. We were in love.' She said that after experiencing marital problems, and one of her children suffering a serious illness, she turned to Billy for support. He was, she claimed, a willing partner who had made it clear to everyone that he fancied her.

1998

Did they give a monkey's?

Social workers in Glasgow were unable to stop the shocking abuse of a young girl. But they did manage to save the family's pet monkey!

Heroin addicts James Barr (40) and Karen Leask (36) were each jailed for five years for the shocking neglect of a 5-year-old girl, a crime Lord MacLean described in Glasgow High Court as 'revolting'. While the judge slammed the pair for their 'total abdication' of responsibility, he was also astonished by the complete inability of social workers to protect the child.

Following an accident in June 1998, when a car knocked the girl down near her home in Easterhouse, she suffered a broken leg and collarbone and was put in a plaster cast. However, while Barr and Leask were high on drugs, they left the child lying in agony and filth in the two-bedroom flat for months on end.

Although social workers visited the squalid property no less than eighteen times, they only gained entry on four occasions and saw the girl only once when they were told she was going back into hospital to have the cast removed. Staff at Yorkhill hospital alerted the girl's general practitioner when she did not attend an appointment to have the cast removed. A health visitor was dispatched to the flat and was told the girl would return to hospital, but made no further checks.

On 20 August, social worker Mary McHugh and a colleague visited Barr and Leask. They failed to see the girl, who was not under social work supervision at the time although her two sisters were. But they did see a 'dirty and smelly' pet monkey running around the flat and alerted SSPCA inspectors. The wretched girl, who had not been bathed for a year, and had numerous bedsores, was eventually rescued by relatives in 1999, following Barr's arrest for another offence. Her plaster cast, which contained cutlery and pens used to scratch her leg ulcers, was removed *ten months late.* Although the girl was properly fed, she was unable to stand up due to wasted leg muscles, her rank hair was full of lice and she was permanently scarred.

As public anger mounted, Glasgow City Council claimed that the child's ordeal wasn't their responsibility but admitted that the case highlighted a 'breakdown of communication' between social workers, health staff and police. However, the Scottish Executive was 'extremely concerned' and asked the council for a full report. Barr's sister called for McHugh to be suspended and it was reported that the social worker was off sick. It was also revealed that social workers wanted to return the girl to Barr and Leask, but this crazy plan was abandoned when they were convicted.

In March 2000, Barr was sentenced to a further two years in jail for dealing in heroin from the Easterhouse flat.

2000

Prison was a holiday camp

Thug Andrew McInnes was let out of prison . . . to go to a holiday camp. McInnes had broken into the house of mill owner Duncan Kelly along with his older brother. They kicked Mr Kelly, punched him on the head and stabbed him five times. Originally charged with attempted murder, 19-year-old McInnes was jailed for five years at the High Court in Kilmarnock in April 1993.

But such is the hold that do-gooders have on our prison system that, after only eighteen months in Dumfries young offenders' institution, he was allowed to go on a rehabilitation course at Butlin's Wonderwest World in Ayr. McInnes was one of ten young people from Dumfries sent to 'Ayr 94 Inspiring Young People'. At Butlin's, the young ned had the chance to take part in water-sports, aerobics and horse riding. And at night the bars were open for drinking and socialising.

Prison bosses said it was common for prisoners to be let out for rehabilitation purposes but they did not often get sent to holiday camps. The Prince's Trust, which organised the trip, said it would continue to take prisoners to Butlin's and denied it was a soft option. Predictably, victim Duncan Kelly had a different point of view. He said, 'He should have been sent to a concentration camp and not a holiday camp. I am disgusted.'

1994

Party on

It was a very elegant affair. The happy couple had just announced their engagement and threw a lavish party for eighty of their closest friends. There was a specially baked cake, a lavish vegetarian buffet and a disco. And a lone piper in full Highland regalia had been hired to play traditional Scottish music.

Nothing strange or startling there. Except that the party was organised by one of Scotland's most notorious criminals and was taking place inside Barlinnie prison in Glasgow. For the fiancé in question was none other than William 'Toe' Elliot, a violent gang boss and drug dealer who was serving life for murdering a pusher who had tried to cheat him on a heroin deal in 1983.

But it was all change now for the bold Toe. He had been influenced by his attractive fiancée, divorcee Ruth Stone (29), who worked for a prison charity. His cell was a testament to his new outlook on life: it had a Mackintosh-style fireplace, shelves with new books and classical music CDs. Elliot (46) had also written plays and produced sculptures.

Guests enjoyed the relaxed atmosphere. A mother of one of the inmates said: 'Once you were in the prison, security wasn't tight. All you needed to say was you were a friend of Toe's and you got in.' One of those friends was fellow murderer and Special Unit inmate Jimmy Boyle, who drove off from the bash in his BMW.

It seemed that Toe Elliot and the other inmates in the Special Unit were denied few of life's little luxuries. It was reported that Ruth Stone spent hours in his cell during visits: 'They are like a couple of starry-eyed youngsters, always cuddling' said one observer.

1991

Bomber's life of luxury

Abdelbaset Ali Mohmed al-Megrahi, who was jailed for life for the bombing of a Pan-Am airliner over Lockerbie in Dumfriesshire in 1988, has the pleasant prospect of living the life of Riley in Barlinnie prison until his expected release in 2028. These special arrangements are expected to cost the Scottish taxpayer at least £5.5 million – on top of the £15 million paid by the Scottish Executive towards al-Megrahi's £75 million trial at Kamp van Zeist in the Netherlands.

Relatives of the 270 Lockerbie victims were furious when it was revealed that 51-year-old al-Megrahi has the exclusive use of four luxurious rooms. He has a kitchen, en-suite bedroom, computer room and a television room with cable television and a collection of videos. He also has a selection of books and receives regular deliveries of fresh food. Even the bars on his cell windows can be discreetly hidden behind curtains.

During his trial, the Scottish Prison Service hinted that a deal with the Libyan government included an agreement on al-Megrahi's future treatment in jail. But Tory MSPs branded the situation 'unacceptable'. And many victims' families felt the same way: Paul Hudson of New Jersey, whose 16-year-old daughter Melina perished in the disaster, said: 'It is not prison and it is not punishment. If he is in prison for mass murder, he should be put in with other prisoners and given the same treatment they are.'

Meanwhile, al-Megrahi's wife and five children live in an exclusive Glasgow suburb in a fully furnished, luxury home rented by the Libyan government, so that they can make regular prison visits. The house is equipped with floodlights, motion detectors, closed-circuit television and a group of burly Libyan security men.

It has to be said that there are many people with serious doubts about al-Megrahi's guilt, among them Robert Black, a law professor at Edinburgh University, who 'cringes' at the lack of evidence. As the head of security at Libyan Arab Airlines, al-Megrahi was only a mid-ranking operative and some people believe his incarceration was purely a political move. Since his conviction, Libya has 'admitted' responsibility for the bombing and United Nations sanctions against the country have been lifted. We may never know the truth.

2003

Frisky Tuckers bonked all night in Sex Block H

Randy Fiona Tucker (29) just couldn't go without nookie when hubby James (32) was jailed for a year on minor drug charges.

Luckily for her he was sent to Castle Huntly open prison near Dundee, which seems to have the doziest screws in Scotland.

It was on Fiona's third visit that the opportunity arose. 'We went for a walk in the grounds which you're allowed to do. There's a big area of bushes and we just darted in. We came out half an hour later feeling a damn sight better. It was fantastic and very exciting that we could have got caught.'

But she decided to go one better and actually spend nights in the nick, which is nicknamed Castle Cushy. Her disguise was his jogging trousers and big jacket, which disguised her shape and made her look like a man. Then she tucked her hair down the jacket and put on a baseball cap. During night inspections she hid under his bed.

Although James shared a cell, other cons swapped to give them privacy and she was able to spend three nights in a row inside the jail. During the day the warders were so taken in by her disguise that she was able to walk around undetected. Fiona claimed that other wives were up to the same tricks and that the jail should have been renamed Sex Block H.

She only got caught when a jealous con reported her to the guards. Her hubby was put in solitary, given another twenty-eight days and sent back to Saughton prison in Edinburgh where he had started his sentence.

1997

Evil cluckers

The cons at Low Moss prison near Glasgow needed to do something to ward off the tedium of life inside. So they devised a ritual called the 'chicken run', which became a tradition in the nick. It was aimed at prisoners who had picked on children or old people.

One of those who endured it was Thomas Binnie (25) who had been sentenced to six months for snatching a bag from an old lady. Binnie was forced to imitate a chicken while running naked with a burning newspaper inserted into his anus. In the course of a six-hour ordeal he was also forced to drink urine and was burned with a cigarette lighter. Just in case he didn't get the message that the other prisoners didn't like him he was then butted, punched and kicked.

Two prisoners at Low Moss were later found guilty at Glasgow Sheriff Court of assaulting Binnie. The prison doctor, Ian Carrie, told the court the chicken run had gone on for years and was difficult to stamp out because of the layout at Low Moss.

1990

8

Just plain crazy

There are some stories that defy categorisation. They're just plain crazy!

Your fart's rotten

Ian Smith put the wind up his opponents when he was playing snooker. So much so that he got a letter from his club secretary telling him he could be banned.

The problem was that every time Ian bent down to play a shot he inadvertently farted. That led to a warning letter from Hugh McCashey, secretary of the Arbroath and District British Legion club. Hugh was keen to clear the air: 'A complaint was raised against you as regards breaking wind on a regular basis in the company of not only male members but also in front of women members. This will not be tolerated and more stringent action will be taken if you continue to do so.'

Ian said, 'I do have a problem. Someone told me it could be caused by chewing gum so I am going to stop using it when I'm playing.'

1990

They wanted a killer

Forty students at Glasgow Caledonian nominated brutal killer Winston Silcott for the honorary presidency of their 'university'. Silcott was jailed for the murder of boxer Anthony Smith in 1986. He was also convicted of killing PC Keith Blakelock during the Broadwater Farm riots in Tottenham but later cleared on appeal. The students said they chose Silcott as a 'victim of injustice'. In the election that followed Silcott got 173 votes; the winner, an anti-apartheid campaigner, received 531 votes.

I am sure that Glasgow Caledonian, a Mickey Mouse university if there ever was one, is proud of its students.

1996

Arrested development

Women civilians who worked for Strathclyde police looking after female prisoners had great difficulty with basic intelligence tests. In fact, only one of the forty staff actually passed.

The questions were hardly Mensa standard and included the following:

- Pairing up words like car and garage
- And plane and hangar
- Doing simple sums

The tests were ordered after their turnkey jobs were changed to include tasks like computer work and the women faced the sack after failing to come up to scratch. One woman said, 'Most of us have been out of school for years and aren't used to exams. Our minds went blank.'

They were probably educated at Glasgow Caledonian University.

1996

He rocked the boat

Jolly fisherman Freddie Wiseman was thrown off a luxury cruise liner for laughing too much. It happened only five days into his twelve-day, £1,750 cruise on the liner *Oriana*.

Freddie (56) was having a whale of a time in the ship's Lords Tavern bar but his loud laughing led to complaints from fellow passengers. So the six foot two, eighteen-stone prawn fisherman was made to walk the plank in Las Palmas, Gran Canaria.

Freddie had to pay for his own accommodation in Las Palmas. Although the *Oriana's* owners – P & O – paid for him to fly to Heathrow, poor Freddie had to stump up for a flight to Inverness and other travel costs.

Freddie said: 'It was unbelievable. Even now, I can hardly think it happened. The captain told me my laughter was upsetting the passengers so I'd have to leave. What did they want me to do? Take anti-laughing pills?'

1997

Heart sick

Staff on cruise liner SS *Edinburgh Castle* asked a man who suffered a heart attack to sign a £672 medical bill minutes after he collapsed. Tom Peters (64), of Prestonpans, just managed to sign the document before he was whisked off to hospital on Corsica.

Tom, his partner Margaret Graham and their friends John and Isabella Mulgrew were on a thirteen-night Mediterranean cruise on the notorious ship (which previously had to be disinfected when passengers caught Legionnaire's Disease). They paid £653 each for the dream holiday but halfway through it turned into a nightmare when Tom developed the symptoms of a heart attack. Medical staff attended but, before being taken ashore, he was asked to sign the bill, which included £70 for night consultation, £160 for heart monitoring and £90 for two heart tests.

Tom later said 'When they gave me the bill, I was so shocked I almost had another heart attack' and John Mulgrew said it was disgusting to give a seriously ill man a medical bill. Jack Waters, a director of the ship's owners, English-based Lowline Ltd, made an unreserved apology saying that the bill should not have been presented. The party was properly insured and only a £100 excess had to be paid.

1998

Pizza nonsense

We all know how much Americans can eat. But the appetites of three Yanks were so gargantuan that they were thrown out of Pizza Hut's restaurant in Glasgow's Argyle Street.

The golfing tourists ordered the all-you-can-eat buffet specials at £5.49 a head. Supersize pizzas are left on hotplates for diners to help themselves and most manage three or four slices, as well as side orders of pasta and so on. But the greedy hogs managed to guzzle three 12-inch pizzas each as well as numerous helpings of the side dishes – the equivalent of ten meals each. When they came back for more, staff decided enough was enough.

A shocked waiter said: 'These guys were typical Americans . . . with typical huge appetites. I don't know if they were actually very hungry or just greedy but the decision was made to ask them to leave. They did put up a bit of resistance but we were left with no option.'

2004

Not oven ready

There is no denying that Robert Ingles was a big guy. He weighed thirty stones, to be precise. But when the Cumbernauld man died after a heart attack, his grieving widow Norma was shocked when Dalnottar crematorium in Clydebank wouldn't accept him because he was too large to go in their furnace.

Norma tried everywhere, even the crematorium in Dunfermline, reputed to have the biggest oven in Scotland. But the body was still two inches too big. And a funeral was out of the question as Robert (57) had begged Norma to ensure he was cremated. He even had a clause inserted in his will specifying that he was not to be buried. 'He had a fear about being buried with lots of beasties crawling all over him' explained Norma and told her: 'Put me in the big, bad fire but don't put me in the bin.'

Just when it seemed he would have to be taken over the water to a Belfast crematorium to find an oven that was big enough, Masonhill crematorium in Ayr said that it could accommodate Robert's massive corpse.

2004

The human fireball

Raymond Doolan turned into a human fireball and died after sniffing petrol. He got some of the petrol on his clothes and, when he lit a cigarette, his clothes caught fire.

The tragedy happened as the freckle-faced 14-year-old and two pals skipped lessons at Lanark Grammar School and went for a walk in Castlebank park. The three boys went into a hut and had a 'buzzy' session, sniffing fuel they found in a lock-up. When his two pals left the hut Raymond lit up and, when he started screaming in terror, they turned round to see him in flames. The boys could do nothing to help and saw their friend die in agony.

Raymond was so badly burned that police had to check his dental records to make a positive identification. A sad end to a young life.

1988

I hear you knocking . . .

When Scot Andrew de Vries chapped his door in the middle of the night, Jeffrey Agee did what any normal Texan would have done. He shot him dead.

De Vries (28) was an oil executive from Aberdeen working in Houston. After a night out in the city he and his colleague Sydney Graves ended up in the home of two men they had met in a bar. Their new acquaintances agreed to drive them back to their hotel but de Vries had been agitated all night. He developed fears – which were perhaps irrational – that the two men were going to kill him and Graves. He made several attempts to get out of the car. Eventually he succeeded and found himself in an upmarket neighbourhood of Houston.

Followed by Graves, he rang the bells of several houses before coming to Jeffrey Agee's place. He knocked on the door, shouted 'call the police' and within seconds was fatally wounded by two shots.

What De Vries could not have known was that the area he found himself in was a burglary blackspot. Due to the level of violence recent break-ins were known as home invasions, in which burglars battered down doors, tied up occupants and stole valuables. Understandably, residents were extremely nervous about intruders.

A Texas grand jury decided not to indict Jeffrey Agee, a geologist, and he faced no criminal charges. The de Vries family felt there had been a cover-up and that Agee's story had many discrepancies. However, Agee paid de Vries's widow £180,000 in an out-of-court settlement when she sued him.

1994

Up shit creek

After six months trudging round Europe looking for work Lawrence Tervit was desperate to get home. The only problem was that the 46-year-old Scot didn't have the £5 fare for the Calais–Dover ferry. So he made the foolhardy decision to cross the Channel on a wooden pallet.

He had walked the six miles south to Sangatte where he found the pallet and quickly knocked up a very basic raft. When his first attempt failed after an hour because of strong currents, Tervit – this time watched by a large crowd, many of whom told him he was crazy – set off again. The first twelve hours on his tiny six-feet-by-three-feet raft were uneventful, but then disaster loomed.

He later recalled what happened next:

> I became exhausted and fell asleep. I was woken up an hour or two later by the loud thudding of an engine. It was dark but I looked up and saw the huge bow of a super-tanker looming before me. I shouted 'oh shit'. I thought I was a goner. I was terrified. I tried desperately to paddle away. The bow wave hurled me out of the ship's path, but it was so powerful my raft flipped over. I thought I'd die. All I could think about were my children. I thought I'd never see them again . . . I seemed to be under the water for an age.

Fortunately for him he was able to swim back to the raft, but only after he had four of his teeth knocked out when his head 'hit something hard'. Reacquainted with his 'vessel', he paddled furiously for three or four hours but still drifted into the main navigation lanes. When he heard the loud blasts from ships' horns, he knew he was in grave danger again. Miraculously, he managed to avoid being hit by any of the huge vessels.

Tervit had another lucky break when he was spotted by two yachtsmen who picked him up before passing him on to a lifeboat. He was taken back to Calais suffering from shock, hypothermia and exhaustion. French coastguards, noting that the Channel is one of the busiest shipping lanes in the world, said that what he had attempted was extremely dangerous.

His brave, if ill-advised, adventure attracted a massive amount of press coverage and a national newspaper paid for his train ticket on the Channel tunnel and then onto his home in Portsmouth. His nearest and dearest were not so forgiving. His sister Pauline called him a 'prat on a pallet' for deserting his four teenage children without telling them, or his ex-wife, where he was going. It also turned out he had only phoned his worried family once during his six months away. Originally from Stoneyburn in West Lothian, Tervit was a graduate of Stirling University, but had been unable to find work in the UK.

1997

Thick as thieves

A building society raider made an astonishing series of mistakes, Edinburgh High Court was told. The 23-year-old Edinburgh man stared at a security camera in the Alliance & Leicester building society on South St Andrew Street, which later provided police with pictures used to identify him. The bungling robber, who refused to be served until all other customers had left, then presented his demand note which was written on the back of a job-application form, complete with his personal details including date of birth, former school and hobbies.

The note read: 'This is a stick up. Put the monney in the bag and dont try enneything. Ive got a gun in my pocket and it aimid at you.' The man, who only pretended to be armed, escaped with £834 but he was arrested nearby shortly afterwards and £825.40 was recovered. Lord Kirkwood sentenced him to thirty months in prison.

1990

S-S-S-S-S-Stick em up

A robber with a speech impediment took so long to say, 'Give me the money' that the police arrived while he was still on the premises.

Three women cashiers at a William Hill bookies in Ibrox, Glasgow couldn't make sense of stuttering Thomas McPherson (40) as he tried to rob their shop and security-camera footage showed punters walking around the shop unaware that a hold-up was in progress. Eventually, frustrated McPherson climbed onto the counter and banged on the anti-bandit screen as he tried to make himself understood. The cashiers suddenly realised they were being threatened, and pressed the alarm.

At Glasgow High Court, the prosecution said that McPherson told the women: 'If you don't open the drawer and give me the money, you are going to get it.' Although staff handed over £341, police arrived with CS gas canisters and batons while he was still in the shop.

McPherson, care of Barlinnie prison, admitted the robbery. He had seven previous convictions for assault and robbery and was on parole from a five-year conviction when he robbed the bookie's. Trial judge Lord Carloway sentenced him to a further six years inside.

2003

Thugs used crippled Billy for knife-throwing practice

At a criminal trial, Edinburgh Sheriff Court was told that Douglas Thomson was dating William MacPhee's former girlfriend when she complained to him that MacPhee was harassing her. So, Thomson and his ex-soldier pal Barry Milligan decided to pay MacPhee a late-night visit following a drinking session. MacPhee, who has multiple sclerosis and requires walking sticks, opened his door when he heard knocking but the two cowardly thugs burst in and frogmarched him through the house. Thomson punched MacPhee repeatedly and cut his telephone wires. Milligan threatened to torch his car (with MacPhee inside) and performed repeated mock drownings on the victim in his bath.

An hour into his five-hour ordeal, a downstairs neighbour reported a leak to the police, which was in fact an overflow from the water torture in the bathroom above. When police arrived at his door, MacPhee told the officers there was nothing wrong while the two thugs hid inside.

The sickening violence, which included MacPhee being used for knife-throwing practice, petered out at 8 a.m. when the effects of the drink wore off. MacPhee was too scared to go to hospital or report the brutal incident but, a week later, a doctor saw his bruised body and the police were informed.

Milligan and Thomson were convicted of the attack and sentenced to eighteen months and two years respectively. MacPhee, from Gorebridge in Midlothian, said: 'I kept thinking it would all be over but instead they just kept on hour after hour . . . I thought they were going to kill me – I really thought I was a goner.'

2000

A good deed

Scots firm Caledonia Square Inch Land cashed-in on the popularity of the BBC series *Monarch of the Glen* by selling off one-square-inch plots of Speyside land at £40 a time. The sale targets buyers from America who are desperate to own a bit of land to cement links with the old country.

The company bought three acres of grazing land near Nethy Bridge in the Highlands and, with eighteen million square-inches for sale, there's enough to raise £800 million. The website offers punters a 'unique Land Deed, traditionally designed with specially commissioned illustrations, individually numbered and with legal terms in English and Gaelic'. Prices are $56.70 for a deed in a presentation tube or $89 for a framed deed.

Company director John Monaghan defended the sale of the virtually worthless souvenirs and denied it was a rip off. He said that a square inch of land was more of a link with Scotland than anything else he could think of. Monaghan added: 'The whole point is that people will have an attractive document, a certificate of ownership that can hang in their office or home and will be a reference point for people who have an interest in Scotland.'

2002–2004

Shat on from a great height

Edna Ormiston was thoroughly disgusted when she returned home from work and found the front windows, walls, roof, garage and part of the driveway covered in keech! The jobbies had fallen out of the sky onto her house near Galashiels and an aeroplane seemed the most likely culprit. A neighbour touched the substance by accident and discovered it was still soft, but not particularly smelly.

Mrs Ormiston and some neighbours spent over two hours using hoses to clean up. Chemicals in the faeces had tinted the windows blue and paint came off the walls during the cleaning, and a sample was later sent to Borders Council's environmental health department. The incident was reported to the Civil Aviation Authority and they investigated radar records in an attempt to find the errant aircraft, as it is illegal for planes to dump waste over land. Mrs Ormiston looked on the bright side and said: 'It's lucky we were not sitting outside at the time.'

2002

Baby was gaga

Babysitter Scott Dillon was sent to prison for four months after his irresponsible behaviour resulted in a 10-month-old baby swallowing a wrap of heroin. The baby found the paper wrap on a coffee table at Dillon's Fort William home while his 34-year-old mother was at a party. Dillon held the tot upside down and tried to induce vomiting in an unsuccessful attempt to recover the substance. The baby was then rushed 66 miles to Raigmore hospital in Inverness suffering from high blood pressure and a fast pulse but he was released safe and well four days later. The child's mother said she was 'shattered' when Dillon arrived at the party and told her what had happened.

At Fort William Sheriff Court, Dillon admitted exposing the baby to danger by allowing him to eat the heroin but he denied the drugs were his and claimed they belonged to a friend he refused to name. Before he was sentenced, Dillon admitted eight previous convictions.

2000

Every little helps

A former council flat in Colinton Mains Drive, Edinburgh was bought by Elizabeth McIntosh from the former Lothian Regional Council for £27,000. Then, in October 1998, she sold it for £130,000 to England-based property firm, Revival Land Ltd. The firm owned an adjacent site set to be developed as a supermarket and, in a deal that created the world's most expensive real estate, they sold the flat on *the same day* to Tesco for £660,000. The retail giant had no interest in the flat, but wanted a strip of its garden measuring six square metres, which was needed for an access path to the new supermarket. The tiny patch of land could have wrecked the retail giant's plans to build the new store.

Although Mrs McIntosh missed out on an extra £530,000

she had no complaints: 'I didn't know how much the house was sold on for and I don't think it's got anything to do with me.'

In August 2000, Tesco offered the flat to buyers for offers over £39,950. Yes, every little helps.

2000

Climb every mountain

A disabled man reached the top of Ben Nevis – in his wheelchair! Despite gale-force winds and mist proud John Barratt (41), an ex-miner from Staffordshire, made it to the summit with the assistance of twenty colleagues from volunteer organisation, the Lions Club, and they celebrated with a bottle of champagne.

The party had attempted the climb in 1986, but they only got halfway before the wheelchair handles sheared off due to metal fatigue. For the successful ascent, scaffolding poles were fixed to the wheelchair for added strength. John protected his hands with rolls of sticking plaster, then propelled himself up the rocky path and was carried by his pals over the most difficult sections.

The ascent took five-and-a-half hours and the downward trip took an hour less. John, who was confined to a wheelchair in 1974 due to a mining accident, said: 'It was really tough going. We are all absolutely exhausted but delighted at our success.' It was a case of triumph over adversity and John and his pals managed to raise around £2,000 through sponsorship for the Royal Commonwealth Society for the Blind.

1987

Making a meal of it

Following a meal in a restaurant, a Glaswegian discovered he had lost his money, so he took two knives from the table and raided a payphone on the premises to pay the bill. Glasgow District Court was told that the 32-year-old was found hiding in the toilet with the stolen cashbox and his pockets bulging with coins. An agent said the accused had a bad record for dishonesty. He lived with a girlfriend and had claimed income support while on a training course that paid him an extra allowance. After receiving the allowance, he went out drinking and ended up in the Ramana restaurant in Sauchiehall Street. He admitted forcing open the payphone and stealing £90 and two knives, and was fined £475.

1991

Package holiday with a difference

Dutch firm Kamstra Travel sold package holidays in Glasgow to business executives. Nothing unusual in that, except that they had to sleep rough under cardboard boxes on the city streets. The holidays were advertised to parties of six or more as an alternative to conventional team-building trips, such as paint balling or mountaineering.

For an all-inclusive price of £450, the businessmen got a cardboard box near soup kitchens in Glasgow's rundown Govan district for two nights. A survival guide with tips on how to mix with genuinely homeless people without being discovered was included. The groups had to work together to survive on the street, but they weren't allowed any money and got a 'typical homeless breakfast' of cold tea and four-day-old bread. The travel firm even handed out musical instruments for them to busk with.

The poverty industry was quickly on the case and described the bizarre holidays as a cynical ploy to exploit the homeless. A spokeswoman for Shelter Scotland said: 'I fail to see what pretending to be homeless is going to teach you. Why should businessmen be competing with homeless people for services? Most people would be disgusted if they knew the person standing next to them in the queue for the soup kitchen could afford to buy the whole unit, never mind the soup.'

In his defence, Bart Jansen, director of Kamstra Travel, said: 'People who normally dress in suits and spend the day in front of a PC will open their eyes and see that it is a tough world out there. People often have a romantic notion about street life and this will let them see how hard it really is.'

2001

The wee swally that went wrong

Robert Gill (23) from Cupar was having a pint in his local, Preston's bar, when he saw a mate perform his party piece – putting a pool ball in his mouth and then regurgitating it. Anything you can do thought Robert . . . and he promptly stuck a ball in his own gub.

But he may just have had a smaller mouth than his pal and he quickly got into difficulty. One witness said it looked as if he was trying to swallow the ball, but this may have been a reflex action when he couldn't get it back out. The publican and his pals took him out of the packed pub and desperately tried to pull the ball out of his throat. But it was all to no avail and Robert died before the ambulance arrived ten minutes later.

1987

The thoughtful terrorists

Two Scots hiking in the Himalayas were robbed at gunpoint by Maoist rebels. But the rebels insisted on giving the trekkers a receipt . . . so that they wouldn't be robbed again further up the trail.

John McNicoll and Ewen Ferguson from Stirlingshire – who were taking part in a charity hike in Nepal – were tucking into dinner in their tent when the men burst in brandishing AK47 machine guns. The terrorists demanded 1,000 rupees from each man; the equivalent of £10.

John McNicoll explained what happened: 'The attackers were armed to the teeth and shouting at us, but we couldn't understand a word they were saying until our guide intervened. He talked with them and then told us that they were demanding 1,000 rupees from each of us. . . . The guide advised us to pay the money because he couldn't guarantee our safety if we argued. Apparently the receipt is so that, if you get set upon again during your trip, you can show it so you won't have to pay twice.'

After paying the money the Scots were able to complete their walk in peace. Although the Maoists are engaged in a bloody campaign to get rid of Nepal's monarchy, they are always very polite to foreigners.

2004

Shetland's Walter Mitty

Chris Readings, formerly of Lerwick in Shetland, developed an unhealthy interest in the emergency services after watching coastguard helicopters bring patients ashore from oil rigs. He acted out his strange 999 fantasies by driving around Shetland with a blue light attached to his car roof.

When his mum Beattie won £900,000 on the National Lottery, she forked out £100,000 for Readings to buy a house in London's Abbey Wood district. Readings (33), his wife and son headed for the city and he blew wads of cash on a fleet of private paramedic-style vehicles. They included a £40,000 ambulance, a £23,000 Rover 800 and a luxury Pan European motorbike worth £10,000, all with yellow-stripes identifying them as emergency vehicles. Readings, who sneered at low-paid emergency workers, had no medical training so he could be arrested for assault if he ever attempted to treat a patient. Police pulled him over on several occasions but his fleet, sirens and flashing blue lights were perfectly legal and the vehicles were properly registered.

Emergency workers raged at his antics as the sham ambulanceman paraded around the ruins of Soho's Admiral Duncan pub following a bombing. A spokesman said: 'We can only assume he was using a scanner to get there so quickly.'

1999

Phone home, ET

UFO expert Graham Wylie opened a telephone helpline to counsel people claiming to have been kidnapped by aliens. Wylie, from Dundee, ran the service from home and looked after his kids while his wife went out to work. He believed aliens called Greys were attempting to take over the world, and says he was also abducted by an alien named Josef who later fed him details of the planned takeover. A dozen calls a month were received from people responding to ads in local papers, apparently from victims who were traumatised by close encounters with little grey men. He charged from £4 to £15 for 'psychic healing sessions'.

1997

Rank bad taste

The car in which two criminals were found murdered turned up again on the mean streets of Glasgow, licensed as a taxi. The victims, Bobby Glover and Joe 'Bananas' Hanlon, were found shot dead in the front seats of the Ford Orion in 1992. The car was being used by Mac's Cabs in the East End of Glasgow, whose office was just a few miles from where the two men were killed.

They had been killed on the same day that rival gangster Arthur Thompson junior was buried. Glover and Hanlon, friends of hard man Paul Ferris, were known enemies of the so-called Licensee, Thomas McGraw. Ferris later claimed his friends were murdered by London hitmen and that their bodies were taken to McGraw's Barlanark pub, the Caravel, before being dumped in Shettleston. The Caravel was demolished hours before detectives turned up to look for clues.

Police spent months examining the car but it was released the following year and sold by a credit company. A friend of Glover's mum Kathy said: 'It's sick. The family say the car should be blown up and not used to ferry people around. They are very angry.' The men's killers were never found.

1996

Neighbour died in freak crash

A woman died in a bizarre head-on collision with a neighbour – 80 miles from home. School secretary Christina Owens (44) was killed instantly when her Toyota hit Douglas Hislop's four-wheel drive Isuzu Trooper on a dangerous section of the A82, four miles south of Fort William. She was returning home to Aberfoyle in Stirlingshire following a visit to her parents' house in Kyle of Lochalsh and crashed into company director Mr Hislop (31), who was inspecting projects for his forestry firm, Scottish Woodlands.

They lived only a few doors apart in identical sandstone cottages, but did not know each other well. Mrs Owens's family was particularly shocked by the strange circumstances of the accident and her husband Paul Owens (56) was taken into hospital after hearing the news. Mr Hislop, who took the incident 'very badly', recovered at home following treatment for bruising, whiplash and broken ribs. A pet dog called Eppie escaped from Mrs Owens's wrecked car but was found safe and well eight days later.

1999

Death slide

David Mason died of horrific injuries after he attached a climber's karabiner (a snap link with safety closure) to a disused cable-car wire then tried to slide down using only his hands for control. Several bystanders tried to stop him attempting the crazy stunt near Canazei in the Marmolada area of the Italian Alps. On the way down, the 49-year-old from Rutherglen lost his grip, collided with rocks several times and smashed at high speed into a pylon 600 feet below. His 18-year-old son Douglas saw the horrific incident and a helicopter later took David to hospital, but he was found to be dead on arrival. A local *carabinieri* spokesman said an investigation into the 'very unusual and bizarre accident' had been launched.

2002

Pulped by walkway

Academic Sarah Callan was on a moving walkway in Rome's Tiburtina railway station when a large hole appeared and she fell into the cogs underneath. She was quickly pulped to death by the powerful machinery. Although commuters had reported the faulty walkway two hours earlier, workmen had only just started repairs when it collapsed. One tourist said that a railway worker tried to help her but he was also pulled in and one of his legs became trapped. A railway spokesman said that it was too early to determine whether or not the repair work caused the woman's death, but the Italian prosecutor's office confirmed that an investigation was under way.

Her ex-husband Jack Baldwin, who she was visiting in Rome, witnessed her grisly demise and was treated for shock. Ms Callan (62), originally from Coatbridge, was known as Sally Baldwin at the University of York, where she had been the popular director of the social policy research unit.

2003

You can take it with you

Gangster Stewart 'Specky' Boyd, who made a fortune from illegal drugs and extortion in Glasgow's tough Nitshill district, was killed when his Audi coupe crashed head-on with a BMW at 120 miles per hour. The cars exploded on the highway near Malaga on the Costa del Sol and five others died in the same accident.

Boyd was buried at Neilston cemetery in East Renfrewshire, and he took a few home comforts with him. A machete, a magnum of champagne and a gram of cocaine were placed in his coffin, perhaps as gifts for the man upstairs! The coffin was decorated with extravagant floral wreaths, and it was a funeral fit for a pharaoh. Although hundreds of people turned up for the interment, a police helicopter circled overhead to keep an eye on the proceedings and many gangland figures stayed away.

It is believed that Boyd ordered the deaths of several people who dared to cross him. One was said to be drug addict Charles Devlin, who was murdered in 1994 with a mixture of heroin and rat poison after moving in with one of Boyd's ex-lovers. Apart from an eighteen-month jail sentence for intimidating a witness, Boyd was able to act with impunity in Scotland. His spectacular demise occurred when he went to Spain to confront a drugs baron who sold him ten kilos of Colombian cocaine for £80,000. The consignment was contaminated by wood dye from new doors used to conceal the drugs and it is thought that the foreign criminals assassinated Boyd.

2003

Beached whale

When forty-stone Linda Early (39) couldn't get up from the bedroom floor, her doctor had no alternative but to call an ambulance to her home in the East End of Glasgow. However, because she was so disgustingly obese, the operation to remove her from the ground-floor flat took five hours. The ambulance crew of four was unable to lift her incredible bulk, so a five-man team from Strathclyde fire brigade was called in and she was eventually wheeled-out of the flat on a trolley. Council-tax payers footed the mammoth £3,000 bill for the rescue, which included a ramp that workmen built up to the front door using a JCB mechanical excavator. The rescuers also had to use a specially reinforced minibus to take her to hospital.

The blimp's legs were barely able to support her massive bulk and she was detained in Glasgow's Royal Infirmary for eight days. She said that she hadn't left her flat for over a year and had trouble reaching the bathroom. Early blamed her horrific problem on sexual abuse she suffered as a child and described her life imprisoned in blubber as a 'living hell'. She admitted she was brought up on a diet of pie and chips but said that, because she rarely moved, she actually ate very little (pull the other one Linda).

After instructing her lawyer to launch legal proceedings against the health service and Glasgow City Council social workers for 'neglecting her care', the local NHS trust looked at the options available to treat her. In December 2000, BBC television featured Linda on *Frontline Scotland* and revealed that she was receiving round-the-clock care costing £900 per week.

2000

Tommy livered life to the full

When Tommy Eldridge (51) was told in November 2000 that he had liver cancer and was expected to die within six months, he decided to throw his own wake on St Patrick's Day. He even hired a horse and cart and a jazz band as the party went on a pub crawl around Burntisland in Fife. At the Golf Tavern, a favourite watering hole, barman Chick Docherty took Tommy's measurements for his coffin and drinkers carved his birth date and a question mark on the lid. Tommy headed off for Majorca with his three kids immediately after the wake, saying 'Life's too short and I'm out to enjoy myself.' That's the spirit, Tommy!

2001

9

Politically correct lunacy

Political correctness long ago infected Scotland. In fact, we are probably now the world champions of doublespeak and gobbledegook.

It's Christmas . . . so don't mention Christ

The distribution of a compact disc was banned by a children's hospital because it mentioned the baby Jesus. The CD of traditional festive songs had been recorded by Jane Butters to raise money for Marie Curie Cancer Care and more than 150 copies were donated to the hospital to raise the spirits of children getting care over the festive period. But a spokeswoman for the Royal Hospital for Sick Children in Edinburgh said: 'We could not just hand out the CD. If it went to every child it could cause offence to those who are not Christian.'

The ban was condemned by a prominent Muslim leader, Bashir Maan, who said, 'This is political correctness gone mad. . . . If people want to celebrate then they should have the right, as should minority groups.'

This was not the only assault on Christmas by people who should know better. The Scottish Parliament banned traditional Christmas cards as they might be offensive to other religions. Faithful to its usual standards, the Parliament ruled that the words 'Merry Christmas and A Happy New Year' must not appear on the official cards because they were not 'socially inclusive', whatever that means.

2003

Storm in a B-cup

Council jobsworths in Edinburgh took the unusual step on painting bras on women's naked breasts. It happened when the Grand Ballet of Tahiti arrived in Edinburgh to perform at the council-owned King's theatre. The impresario – Richard Condon – produced publicity material to advertise his show. But he caused outrage among the politically correct brigade . . . because the women on the posters were topless.

Union branch secretary Adam Montgomery sent in a letter of complaint in which he pompously denounced the posters as 'offensive material that was a denigration of women as sexual objects'. A complaint was also made by the council's feared women's committee.

Richard Condon was outraged: 'This is going back to the Dark Ages' he thundered, 'Don't they even know that the women of Tahiti never wear a bra?' But the council was unmoved by his protests and sent out a crack squad of painters to cover up the offending boobs.

1988

Barmy cooncil bans army

Glasgow City Council banned the army from using its land in unemployment blackspots like Easterhouse and Drumchapel. The irony was that the regiment concerned was the Royal Highland Fusiliers, which has traditionally recruited soldiers from Glasgow.

The Fusiliers wanted to put on displays of equipment and high-tech simulators to give youngsters a taste of army life.

A spokesman for the cooncil said, 'It is a matter of the Council recognising the importance of the armed forces but not wanting to encourage blatant militarism.'

1996

Schoolgirl aged 6 branded a racist

Jennifer Claire Whiteside was branded a racist by her school, Mount Florida primary in Glasgow. The 6-year-old allegedly made racist remarks to a Pakistani pupil. The school claimed that the P2 pupil said: 'People who come from Pakistan should stay in Pakistan and not in Scotland.' The next day she allegedly said: 'Pakistanis cause trouble and are always fighting and causing wars.'

Head teacher Lesley Dalgleish wrote to her parents pointing out that racist incidents and remarks in schools now had to be reported. She also asked them, 'to have a chat with the girl and explain how important it is to be careful what she says.'

Understandably her parents were upset and demanded an apology from education bosses. They also pointed out that most of Jennifer's pals were Asian.

This was far from an isolated incident. It turned out that the former Strathclyde Regional Council – a bastion of loony political correctness – had sent out more than one hundred letters to parents accusing their kids of racism.

1990

Golly gosh

Top people's store Jenner's got into trouble for selling golliwogs at Christmas. Despite the fact that the shop had sold them for 156 years, the race relations' industry swung into action in a fit of self-righteousness. Furious race-equality officer, Danny Onifade – who works for something called the Lothian Racial Equality Council – was first to the barricades. He spluttered: 'We hold these toys in abhorrence . . . we think they should be removed from sale immediately. These dolls are a legacy of slavery.' He gave Jenner's three days to stop selling them or else his organisation would picket the store.

But Jenners insisted the shop would keep on selling the

dolls and pointed out that the name 'gollies' was no longer used and had been replaced by the term 'golly dollies'. The controversy certainly did sales no harm at all; three days after the storm broke, Jenners announced it had sold out of the toy and that there was a waiting list for them.

1994

There'll be nae poofs loose aboot this hoose

Tom Forrest caused a furore when he refused to allow two 'sexual deviants' to share a double bed in his Highland guest house. The story was featured prominently in national newspapers and was even the subject of heated debate on BBC Television's *Question Time*.

It all started when homosexual Stephen Nock of London tried to book a double room in the three-star Cromasaig bed and breakfast in beautiful Wester Ross for himself and his boyfriend. Expecting a warm welcome he was surprised to receive the following e-mail from Mr Forrest: 'We do not have a problem with your personal sexual deviation, that is up to you. You are welcome to our twin room if you wish but we will not condone your perversion.' (It is interesting to note that Tom would have let them have a room with two single beds, as if that would have ensured they would not have sex.)

Mr Nock immediately dashed off a complaint to VisitScotland asking the tourist body to remove Mr Forrest's establishment from its website. He was clearly upset by Tom's remarks: 'I was really looking forward to my trip to Scotland and this bigoted attitude was really hurtful.'

But Tom was unrepentant and gave his reasons in greater detail: 'I stand by exactly what I said. I do not go along with this word "gay". They are not happy in that situation. I called them poofs and will continue to call them that. I am not homophobic. I have got friends who are homosexual and they call themselves poofs. I have had bent people come stay with us and they have been nice. But they have been staying in a twin room and they respect our wishes.'

After the incident, Mr Forrest posted a notice on his website saying that only heterosexual couples or single guests would be allowed to stay in double rooms. And he added: 'I am very tolerant but I have received eighty or more abusive e-mails from all these poof organisations, which is turning me against that sort. Gay is a word that means happy to me. I do not try and lift my shirt and I do not lift theirs.'

Although, predictably, VisitScotland removed his establishment from its register of officially recommended places to stay, Tom Forrest's stand seems to have boosted his business. He claimed that the guest house had never been busier and that he had received hundreds of letters of support. One correspondent, Tam, a fellow Scot, was unequivocal in his praise: 'Goan yersell big man, keep those fucking tail gunners out.'

2004

No chinks in the PC armour

A cop was reported to the deputy chief constable of Strathclyde police when he called Chinese people 'chinks' during a lecture to new recruits. Unfortunately for the unnamed 40-year-old detective constable – an expert on criminal intelligence who was talking about the Triad gang menace – one of the rookie bobbies was from a Chinese family and a formal complaint was made. While the officer was probed he was told he could lose his £25,000-a-year job.

Meanwhile, another Strathclyde officer, Kenny Orr, admitted making racist comments in Glasgow's Maryhill police station. In front of a colleague from an ethnic minority background, PC Orr had picked up a propelling pencil and said: 'This is obviously a Paki make – there's hardly any lead in it.' Orr was asked to resign at a disciplinary hearing. However, a few weeks later Chief Constable John Orr (no relation) reinstated the officer following an appeal and a full apology, but he was fined a week's wages (£451) for his indiscretion.

2000

Poetic licence revoked

Kilt-wearing Scots poet Stewart Ainslie was charged with racism when an English couple found one of his nationalist rhymes in their garden.

Mr Ainslie, from Buchlyvie in Stirlingshire, fell over when he visited friends in Milton of Buchanan. He lost his poem – 'For The Gid O' Scotland' – when it was blown away by a strong wind. Ainslie gathered up his other papers but failed to notice that the work was missing.

An English couple next door to his friends found the poem the following day. They took offence and called police, who tracked Mr Ainslie down when they found one of his signed odes on a wall in a garage in nearby Kippen. He was questioned for an hour and charged with acting in a racially aggravated manner! Ainslie was also instructed to keep away from Milton of Buchanan. After eleven months, common sense prevailed. The ludicrous charge was dropped by the procurator fiscal, who decided there would be no further proceedings.

The poet insisted there was nothing sinister about the piece, adding that he doesn't hate the English. The full text reads as follows:

Born brave folks they are north o'
the border,
Suffering at the hons o' the English
order,

Orders that murdered oor Scottish daughter,
Like Culloden, a mindless bloody slaughter,
Lets no let them dae this tae us nae more,
Support the SNP an' show the rest the door,
You know it makes sense . . . !!

2003

Grinch gives Christmas back

Edinburgh City Council officials looked like buffoons following their attempt to ban parents from filming or photographing their children during school performances. The 'nanny state' ruling came to light shortly before Christmas when a parent was prohibited from photographing her son during a school nativity play. Council officials explained that the ban was introduced to prevent paedophiles making movies but failed to produce any evidence of paedophile filmmakers in audiences. It was also noted that Dr Sue Hamilton – the council's child protection officer and one of the people behind the ban – was unknown to real experts in the field.

The council then tried to pass the buck by advising the media to contact police saying it was a matter for them. However, Lothian and Borders police revealed that they had not advised the council to impose the ban and that no incidents of paedophiles filming had ever been reported to them. And, to make matters worse, many councillors revealed that they had not been consulted when officials and education convener Revd Ewan Aitken drew up the rules.

As the furore deepened, one mum fought back and was granted legal aid to take her case against the council to the Court of Session. However, shortly before the case came to court, the council took legal advice and swiftly changed direction. Trendy Church of Scotland minister Ewan Aitken (whom protestors labelled the Grinch after the Dr Suess character who stole Christmas from kids), made a humiliating apology and the ban was lifted.

2002

Silly Qualifications Authority

The Scottish Qualifications Authority admitted that illiterate children are given help to pass exams, including Standard Grade English! An SQA spokeswoman said that if a child had consulted a psychologist and had a record of 'special needs' (which includes the inability to read and write), then help is given to pass exams.

A former English teacher, who resigned over the scandal, explained that a boy who could not read and could only just write his own name was assisted by having someone read out the exam questions and then write down his answers. This particular lad obtained a general level pass for reading and a credit level pass for writing – despite the fact he could do neither. Yet another nail in the coffin of the Scottish educational system.

2000

Talking pollocks

Bob Pollock (62), a lollipop man at Haddington primary school in East Lothian, was used to guiding kids across the road with a helping hand. But the caring world of 'Pop Man' was blown apart when busybodies objected to his friendly neck tickles and pats on the head. Bob was hauled before his East Lothian Council supervisor, who warned him there had been a complaint and that it was best he didn't touch children 'as it could be misunderstood'. Bob was also informed the matter would be entered on his work record; he was so upset he became ill and was signed off work for a month by his doctor.

As angry parents rallied round the popular lollipop man and his disabled wife Mary, it was revealed that a busybody teacher at the school had instigated the complaint. One of the children had innocently told the teacher about Bob's pats and tickles during a classroom talk on 'stranger danger' and the snoop swiftly reported Bob to his bosses.

1997

Spanking teacher booted out

Following two days of hearings, a committee of the General Teaching Council found a 49-year-old Lanarkshire-based teacher guilty of gross misconduct and ruled that he should be struck off the teacher's register.

The decision was a victory for potty child protection campaigners who persecuted a vicious witch-hunt against the man, with no concern whatever for his children. The man, unnamed for legal reasons, had taken his 8-year-old daughter to a dentist in Motherwell on Christmas Eve 1998 but the girl became hysterical and, in front of shocked patients and staff, he pulled down her trousers and knickers and spanked her bare bottom six times. Surgery staff then called the police. In 1999, the man was convicted of assault and admonished, and the sheriff said he had gone beyond the limits of punishment allowed by law. Three of his children were placed under social work supervision and he was given a non-teaching library job.

The man admitted he was wrong to smack his daughter in the waiting room, but said his children were being punished in the cause of political correctness. The General Teaching Council's decision was later overturned at the Court of Session but the man did not return to teaching. In February 2003 he resigned from his non-teaching job at a computer education centre due to his strained relationship with his employer, North Lanarkshire Council.

2000–2003

School dumps aids motto

Teachers at one of Scotland's leading elementary schools, Milngavie primary, were accused of having gone PC mad when they ditched the 125-year-old school motto 'Each Aids The Other', because it included the word 'Aids'.

Head teacher Christine Reid told pupils and parents that there are: 'too many connotations surrounding the word 'Aids'; it seems inappropriate'. She asked pupils to devise a new motto. However, disgusted parents called for the motto to be reinstated and one argued: 'This is political correctness gone mad. To say that the word "Aids" is inappropriate is complete and utter nonsense and I fail to see how anyone would find the word offensive. I am ashamed and embarrassed and I doubt any sensible person would think there was any justification for change.'

2000

10

Big, daft polis

Cops are not known for being the brightest bulbs in the box. Find out why.

He liked a wee drink at the fitba'

John Embleton of Crieff was looking forward to the St Johnstone versus Partick Thistle match at McDiarmid Park, Perth. But, as ever, he found it hard to go for ninety minutes without a drink. And so he made sure he had a bottle of his favourite tipple to hand even though he was contravening the Criminal Justice Act of 1980 that makes it illegal for fans to take bottles into soccer matches. A sensible law given the amount of drink-related violence in Scottish football.

Sure enough, the bottle was spotted by an observant policeman as he made his way into the ground. It was duly confiscated and John was told he could pick it up at the end of the match. It was a real hardship for someone who depended on drink the way that John did.

His parents would be annoyed too. Particularly because John was only five months old and the bottle in question was a soft-plastic container for his milk. It had been sticking out of the jacket pocket of his father, George Embleton, who intended to give his son a feed at half time. After all, John was a bit young for the traditional pie and Bovril.

1989

Ruff justice

It's tough on the mean streets of Scotland, especially for the intrepid police officers who face danger every day of their working lives. It was especially hazardous for WPC Lynn Burns, who was savaged by hellhound Cassie when a workman inadvertently let the beast out of its house in Kilmarnock. The full majesty of the law was brought to bear as police pulled out all the stops to prosecute owner James McManus. Constable Burns and a colleague spent hours on the case and called at the homes of Mr McManus's neighbours to get witness statements. After an investigation lasting several days he and his daughter were charged under the Dangerous Dogs Act, 1991 for failing to keep Cassie under control.

But Cassie was only nine inches tall and weighed less than six pounds. The little Yorkshire terrier had bitten the policewoman on the calf, an attack that hardly qualifies as a savaging by the Hound of the Baskervilles. Even Sheriff Croan, who heard the case in Kilmarnock Sheriff Court, agreed. He told the procurator fiscal that he was astonished Mr McManus had been prosecuted and said: 'I have had a dozen worse bites from my own dog.' Nevertheless the sheriff had no option but to fine Mr McManus £150.

Constable Burns was working as a community officer at the time of her 'ordeal'. What a great job she did to build links with local people. James McManus was understandably embittered by the treatment he received: 'I was recently assaulted by four shoplifters and no one has been arrested. It was amazing the amount of effort put in by the police and the fiscal to convict me for this.'

2004

The PC PCS

In 2004, at a time when crime was going through the roof, loony police chiefs in Lothian and Borders issued a comprehensive guide to politically correct language. Here is the complete guide to the words officers can't use:

- Jump the dyke
- Manhole cover
- Accident blackspot
- Nitty-gritty. It's racist. This well-known phrase is thought to derive from the remains found in the holds of slave ships.
- Rule of thumb. It's sexist. Because it comes from an ancient law that prohibits men from beating their wives with an implement thicker than the thumb.
- Homosexual. It's homophobic. There was allegedly a belief in the nineteenth century that gays suffered from an illness and should be given a pseudo-scientific name. Also banned are expressions like 'he bats for the other side'.
- Old, pet or dear. They're ageist and can be 'devaluing and patronising'. 'Old' is particularly offensive as it 'suggests worn out and of little use'.
- One of the boys. 'Not really appropriate as it implies that, only by behaving like men, can women be accepted by those men in their workplace.'

Attempting to justify this barmy guidance, deputy chief constable Tom Wood of Lothian and Borders Police said: 'We live in very sensitive and dangerous times in terms of language and attitudes and people are very quick to take offence'. Yes Tom, they are. Especially the victims of crime who take great offence at your force's inability to catch criminals. Perhaps it's time you jumped the dyke, became one of the boys and got down to the nitty-gritty.

2004

Miss Scotland, the cops and loony feminists

Strathclyde Police thought they had won a watch when they secured the services of Miss Scotland, Nicola Jolly, to promote

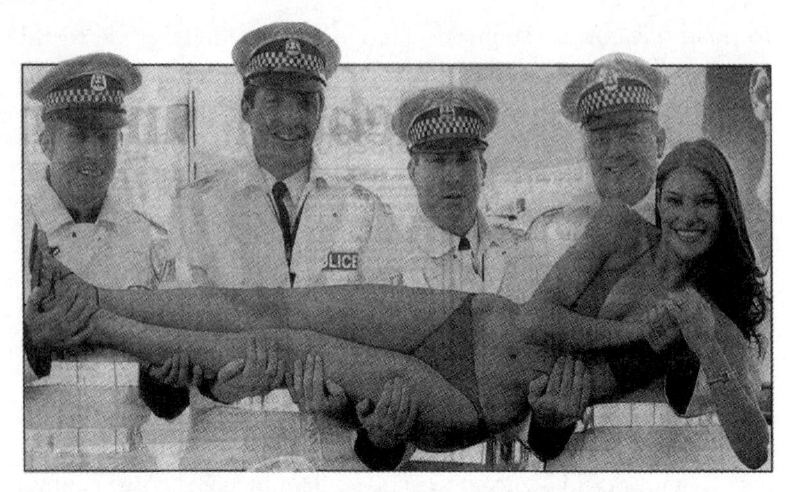

Miss Scotland, Nicola Jolly, with three lucky cops

an initiative targeting the sale of stolen goods. The photo (above) of Nicola being held aloft by four strapping constables was published in *Police Review*. The caption underneath read: 'Officers got their hands on some hot property this week.' The campaign's planners believed that having a fit young woman in her bikini would attract the attention of young males, the main offenders in vehicle theft.

But they reckoned without the monstrous regiment of feminists. Complaints flooded in from women officers and from representatives of the equal opportunities industry. Their spiritual leader, Carole Howlett, deputy assistant commissioner of the Metropolitan police and chairwoman of the Association of Senior Women Officers said: 'It was with dismay and surprise that I read the caption that accompanied the photograph . . . describing her as "hot property" is not only demeaning and insulting, but astounding.'

While Jeremy Wheeler, spokesman of something called the Police Diversity Trainers Network, bleated: 'This is a classic example of why so many female, ethnic minority and gay officers despair.' (Jeremy, I can understand why some females and gays might object, but surely men from ethnic minorities like women too). And, not to be outdone, the Equal Opportunities Commission, weighed in with a ritual protest: 'It is astonishing that any police force would promote itself in such a way in this day and age.'

Such was the volume and ferocity of the complaints that *Police Review* editor, Catriona Marchant, was forced to print an apology.

2003

Armless

Humourless cops in Berwickshire were up in arms about a practical joke played by motorists. It started with clothes being dumped in a lay-by and then a car driving by with a dummy arm hanging out of the boot. The dummy arms were very realistic and consisted of a jacket sleeve, shirt cuff and a hand.

This was followed by 999 calls from gullible members of the public, who thought a murder had been committed. What passes for a major operation in sleepy Berwickshire was mounted: the CID were called in and roadblocks set up. One of the drivers was apprehended and given a severe warning.

A police spokesman later said: 'This bizarre practice must stop. We're on the lookout for these idiots.'

1990

Taking down her particulars

Busty bobby Susan Johnston was at a disadvantage as she tried to arrest crooks in Tayside. Her huge 36G boobs got in the way. 'If I chased anyone down the street I would be sore for two days. Men would see me running along and their eyes would pop out of their heads.'

So she got an operation at Dundee Royal Infirmary on the NHS to try and reduce her massive breasts to a mere 36C: 'I'm not sure what size I'll be when the bandages come off but at least I can see my belly button now.' Well at least she was up front about it.

1995

Shafted

A crack team of officers in a fleet of police vehicles screeched up to a block of flats. Their target: drug dealers in a second-floor apartment. They knew they had to move fast and, ignoring the stairs, seven of them crammed into the lift.

Then . . . nothing. The lift refused to move. And to make matters worse they couldn't get the door open and were stuck in the lift for an hour. Residents in the flats – in Fort Street, Leith – said they heard no cries for help, just muffled sounds from the lift shaft.

When they were finally freed, the sheepish cops had to walk past sniggering tenants. As one tenant said, 'If they were trying for the element of surprise I think they lost it somewhere in the first hour.'

1997

We've got a wee bit of bad news for you!

Ian Findlay was gutted when thieves stole the apple of his eye: a high-performance 150 miles-per-hour Ford Sierra Cosworth. But he cheered up when police used an expensive high-tech tracking device he had fitted to trace, and recover, the car. The whole process had taken only three hours from when the Sierra was stolen in Irvine to its recovery in Coatbridge.

But then Mr Findlay (31), of Ardrossan, got the shock of his life. Police phoned him again and told him that the car had been driven into a tree and was a total write-off. The officer who was driving the car had swerved to avoid another vehicle, gone off the road, run into a ditch and then crashed into the tree.

Ian was understandably upset: 'It was a car I had always wanted. I never had a problem with car thieves. Now I find out it was safer in their hands than with the police.'

1998

Cap that

When three police vehicles screeched up with their sirens wailing in front of a suspicious-looking car in Denny, Stirlingshire, worried onlookers feared that a gun battle was about to erupt. Then the police hauled out four passengers, ordered them to put their hands on the bonnet, frisked them for weapons and searched the car and boot.

But the weapons turned out to be a cap gun and a water pistol that belonged to 3-year-old Craig McLagan and 2-year-old Jennifer McLean. The tots were on their way home from an innocent shopping trip with their parents when their car was stopped. Jennifer's father, Eddie McLean (26), said: 'It was like something on TV. There were about eight officers including two plainclothes men. . . . It was only later they said we were stopped on suspicion of having firearms.'

1989

They made no bones about it

When Alan Duggan and Julie Tanner returned to their burnt-out home to lay a bouquet of flowers in memory of their dead sons, their pilgrimage quickly turned to horror. They discovered remains of a child they thought they had already buried. The couple found a piece of backbone ten inches long and a palm-sized piece of skull with hair attached, which the officers investigating the fire had failed to recover.

Their two boys – 5-year-old Jack and 3-year-old Toby – had been buried in a single coffin only three weeks before. Duggan, an officer with Grampian police, immediately phoned his colleagues but the couple had to wait ninety minutes before the police arrived at Tillyduke schoolhouse in Strathdon, Aberdeenshire. The officers on duty then blithely informed the grieving couple that the remains came from a deer burned by a farmer then dragged to the scene by animals.

However, when the bones were analysed by independent forensic anthropologist, Dr Sue Black of Glasgow University, she immediately realised they were human. Then DNA analysis revealed that the remains belonged to one of the boys. A thorough search of the scene filled thirty small bags with more bones.

It was later revealed that the senior officer who oversaw the original fire investigation wasn't based at the scene but directed operations from his office, 45 miles away in Aberdeen. Tayside police were appointed to lead an inquiry into the handling of the case. The boys' coffin was exhumed following a court order and they were reburied on 17 March, six weeks after the first funeral and two months after the fire. Police representatives were instructed not to attend the service.

The fire had been caused by an electrical fault and Alan Duggan (34) suffered 35 per cent burns in a brave attempt to rescue his two sons from the blazing building. He spent a week in Aberdeen Royal Infirmary and was off work for months following skin-graft operations. Julie Tanner (39) was also badly burned and suffered from shock. Her 12-year-old daughter Micki, who raised the alarm, also survived.

It was later announced that no action was to be taken against any officer of Grampian police.

2000

Nicked . . . at eight miles per hour

Betty Dow was returning home after a trip to feed ducks at Stirling University when she was told 'to get off the road' by cops. But the 73-year-old from Bannockburn was driving a Free Rider electric scooter with a top speed of eight miles per hour!

A spokesman for Central Scotland Police later said that the warning was a 'matter for discretion' and would have been given 'for her own safety'. However, a quick check of the *Highway Code* revealed that Betty, who drove high-performance motorbikes in her youth, had every right to be on the road. Help the Aged spokesman Lindsay Scott said: 'She is qualified and fully entitled to be on the road, so there should be no reason to remove her.' Not unless you're an over-excited policeman who doesn't know the rules, that is.

2003

A date for your diary

The 1999 Scottish Police Federation diary, which is distributed free to around 14,000 officers, contained a full-page advertisement for a kinky wife-swapping brothel opposite the page listing the federation's officials. The advert said: 'While in town for that X-tra special treatment, why not visit Scotland's ultimate health club?'

For a £15 admission fee, the Park Grove House health club in Glasgow offered sunbeds, steam room, sauna, private jacuzzis, spa, massage and a video lounge. Scantily clad women on the premises could also offer off-beat bobbies a couple of little extras: topless hand-relief for £35 and full sex for £60. The dodgy club was also allegedly used for meetings of a group of horny wife-swappers. It is thought that the English company that produced the diary did not realise the true nature of the club.

1999

Cops prevent crib-napping

Police mounted a twenty-four-hour guard on a life-size doll of baby Jesus in Glasgow's George Square – to stop it being stolen! The doll, which featured in a nativity scene as part of the city's Christmas celebrations, had been pinched before. A disgruntled policeman on guard duty said: 'Everyone thinks it's a bit of a joke. But nobody is laughing when they are standing about in freezing conditions for eight hours at a time, being brainwashed with the same Christmas carols as they babysit a plastic doll.'

1999

She kicked up a stink over pink fart

Norman Walker was surprised when a policeman called at his house in Invergarry to discuss a complaint made by a passing lady motorist. She had the wind put up her by the nine-inch-high letters on Norman's wrecked rally car, which lay in his garden by the main road. The lady from Fort William took offence to the F.A.R.T. acronym for Fort Augustus Rally Team written on Norman's pink-coloured Peugeot 205 GTI, and had reported the matter to the constabulary.

Fish-farm worker and rally driver Norman had difficulty believing anyone could object to the lettering, especially as the full name was written underneath. However, the constable told Norman to cover up the vehicle, or remove it. Norman used a tarpaulin to hide the offending letters but he said that the police should watch out: rallying is popular in the area and there are up to twenty FARTs on the road at any one time. A police spokesman later announced: 'The matter is closed.'

2003

They didn't take it on board

Strathclyde's finest rebuffed superiors who asked them to wear sandwich boards advertising an anti-crime initiative and parade around suburban shopping centres in south Glasgow. A chief inspector from Giffnock police station refused to be photographed wearing a set of boards and one officer said the idea was crazy, adding that he joined the force to fight crime and not to be a marketing man.

The rebellion began when police chiefs and East Renfrewshire council officials revealed their latest moves in the Spotlight initiative. Council officers had been told that beat policemen would wear the goofy boards while on duty at shopping centres and had spent hundreds of pounds on having them made. Following the revolt, council employees were told they would have to wear the boards instead, and would be escorted by the conceited constables.

1996

Cops objected to Jim's skean dhu sticking out

When pipe major Jim Motherwell turned up in full Highland dress at Heathrow airport, anxious cops spotted a skean dhu in his sock and an armed response team pounced on the unfortunate Scot.

But 42-year-old Jim explained to the overzealous officers that the knife was part of his national dress. The English policemen were unaware that the skean dhu is exempt from laws that prohibit carrying an offensive weapon. Jim told the bobbies that he was at the airport to meet a friend flying in from Scotland who was due to judge a piping competition at Eton College, where Prince Harry was a pupil. Jim also explained he was a serving soldier and amazed the cops by adding that, as the Queen's personal piper, he played for fifteen minutes outside Her Majesty's window every morning.

The red-faced Old Bill apologised and said that strict airport-security measures meant they had to apprehend anyone looking suspicious or carrying a weapon. A spokeswoman for the Metropolitan police confirmed that a man carrying a skean dhu had been approached, but no offence had been committed and he was not cautioned.

Jim, who hails from Kilsyth in Stirlingshire, has two other

unusual royal responsibilities – he winds the clocks at Balmoral and runs Buckingham Palace's private cinema. He has played the pipes at royal funerals and entertained many VIPs and celebrities, including George Bush senior, Joan Collins, Liz Hurley and former James Bond, Roger Moore.

2003

11

Old gits

The scandalous behaviour of Scotland's pensioners has long been a source of national shame.

They just had to play around

All was well with the world. Jimmy Hogg had just hit a perfect drive on the first hole at his local club. The prowess of the 77-year-old was admired by his four elderly pals as they waited to tee off. But it was all too much for old Jimmy. He promptly collapsed and died of a massive heart attack.

You would be forgiven for thinking that his companions might have abandoned their outing out of respect for an old friend. Not a bit of it. In fact, the original grumpy old men had all played their tee shots before the ambulance taking Jimmy's body away was even out of sight. They then carried on with their round as normal, at Kinghorn golf club in Fife.

As one of the four pensioners – Jack Ketchin – explained: 'It may seem a bit hard-hearted, but he would have done the same.'

1996

An accident waiting to happen

Heidi Beerensson was a kindly old lady who lived for her dogs. A pillar of the community, the 79-year-old retired social worker was respected by everyone who knew her and she helped to raise money for a local dog shelter. Still very active, Heidi liked to get around the fair city of Perth in her tiny Ford Ka.

But gentle Heidi came close to killing two hundred people when she crashed into an express train that was doing 100 miles per hour. She blundered onto a level crossing after swerving round the barrier, which had just been lowered. Somehow she also managed to ignore the loud warning signal that sounds when a train is due. The pensioner later claimed that she was dazzled by the winter sun which was very low in the sky that December morning. Her mistake was very surprising as she had used the level crossing many times before.

The crash happened at the Forteviot crossing on the B934. It is used by the Inverness-to-London express, the train that hit Heidi's car. Miraculously, no one was killed in the collision although a local woman had a lucky escape when a cog from the train's engine flew through her window. The train driver was in shock and had to be replaced by a relief. As for Heidi she suffered only minor injuries, although her car was a write-off.

Heidi was originally charged with dangerous driving but this was reduced to careless driving. She was fined £200 and – thankfully for other road users – banned from driving for two years at Perth Sheriff Court.

2003–2004

Not such sheltered lives

Meals-on-wheels wasn't the only service supplied to OAPs on a sheltered-housing scheme in Saltcoats, Ayrshire. Prostitutes made regular visits to the complex on a Monday: pension day. One of the hookers was bottle-blonde Sharlene Howe (21), who charged the elderly punters £20 a time. Her best customer admitted: 'This is all a bit embarrassing. I did not invite her in but she came in and wanted money and I gave it. She offered sexual favours; well, straight sex.'

But he was not alone. Vice girls were seen going quickly in and out of the homes of other randy male residents. Female tenants in Canal Court were far from happy and one said: 'This used to be a nice area, a place where elderly people came to live a peaceful life. Instead we have nothing but grief.'

Following an investigation Howe was given a police caution.

2004

He gave her the finger

It was Friday the thirteenth, a day that brings bad luck and misfortune. And so it proved for Revd Marjory Macaskill when she found a finger on her porch. The Church of Scotland minister immediately called the police who sent teams of specialist officers rushing to the scene in Cardonald, Glasgow, and cordoned off local streets while searching the area for more body parts.

But it turned to be a false alarm. The finger belonged to pensioner Frank McKissock who had sliced off the digit with a power saw. The DIY fanatic had been helping a pal put up a fence when the saw jammed. Old Frank tried to flick the safety guard off but missed and took the finger right off. It flew 100 feet into the minister's garden three houses away and landed on her porch.

Frank (69) was taken to hospital but when he got home the CID called to say they had his finger in a bag of ice and had even taken a fingerprint of it. Frank said they asked him if he recognised it and he replied: 'Yes. That's the one I lost earlier today.' But because it was not found on time, doctors told Frank there was no chance of sewing it back on.

Despite the accident the retired taxi driver was keen to get back to his DIY: 'I'll start back as soon as my stitches are removed next week. I'm going to be helping my daughter renovate her back garden.' Frank, give it up!

2004

Taggart

A sick hoaxer sent a letter to elderly people offering them a part on *Taggart* . . . as a corpse. The letters read: 'We are looking for someone with a natural, sad, haggard expression, deformed torso, misshapen legs and a large bottom. The person will play the part of a murder victim and will be seen for approximately five seconds, naked, face up and in a contorted position on Glasgow Green.'

The letters seemed genuine: they were sent out on forged Scottish Television notepaper, included the words Taggart Productions and contained details about the station and its programmes. STV received many complaints from distressed pensioners and advised recipients of the bogus letter to contact the police.

But they should never have been taken in by the hoaxer. *Taggart* already had a stiff with a natural, sad, haggard expression and a deformed torso. His name was Mark McManus.

1993

No fool like an old fool

Ken Hopes of Edinburgh hadn't had sex for twenty years. His wife Rita was no longer interested and didn't 'want to be bothered'. But she very considerately gave permission for her 71-year-old husband to pay for nookie.

So the bold Ken enlisted the services of call girl Tess Trotter, who visited his house on a Sunday morning when Rita was at church. At first it was all plain sailing. But then Ken made probably the biggest mistake of his life: he lent Tess £2,750 to buy a car. The arrangement was that she would repay him in kind, at £50 per sex session. Although Trotter made nine visits, Ken got suspicious when she failed to turn up three Sundays in a row.

Desperate to get his money back he made many phone calls pleading for the cash. When this approach failed he ended up going to her house in East Lothian to have it out with her. When Tess again blanked him, he rather pathetically let down the tyres on her car.

By this time Trotter was working as a prostitute at the Scorpion sauna near Easter Road and denied all knowledge of Ken and his money. As she said, 'Really, there's no fool like an old fool.'

1995

12

Sectarian madness

Religious hatred has no place in modern Scotland. But someone forgot to tell the bigots.

In the doghouse

Nan O'Malley's dog Mo was one of the most popular mutts in Dumbarton. Nan had named her pet after the Celtic striker Mo Johnston and while he was banging in the goals for the men in green and white, the dog was in clover. People would fuss over him, whistle at him in the street and he was often called Super Mo.

But all that changed in 1989 when Johnston, a Catholic, crossed the Old Firm divide and signed for Rangers after a spell playing his football in France. To add insult to injury, Johnston had initially agreed – in principle at least – to go back to Celtic.

Overnight the canine Mo became a hate figure for Celtic (and many Rangers) supporters. He got death threats. People said they would break his legs. Others advised Nan to have him put down. Even small children would run up to Nan and tell her they didn't like the dog any more. Nan was bemused: 'What kind of mentality do people have?' she wondered. Nan, you may well ask.

1989

A blessing is disguised

Bosses at Gartnavel hospital had to take down a blessing from the Pope after many complaints from visitors. The framed blessing had been put behind the reception desk late on a Wednesday afternoon, but by the Thursday morning it had gone.

The hospital chaplain, Father Brian McNaught, had accepted it on behalf of patients and staff while attending Tom Winning's elevation to Cardinal in the Vatican in November 1994. David McPherson, Gartnavel's director of operational services, said, 'The picture was not meant to offend anyone . . . we are trying to find an alternative place for it.'

1995

We won't teller off

The manager of the Royal Bank of Scotland in Shotts was bemused by a letter from District 32 Orange social club. The club was demanding that a female bank worker be moved to another branch because she wore a crucifix to work. The Lodge felt it would be best all round if she was transferred out of the 'mainly Protestant town'.

The bank – which at first thought the letter was a joke – refused and said the woman would continue to work there.

1995

The chicken-supper rap

A Channel 4 documentary entitled *Football, Faith and Flutes* highlighted the bigotry prevalent in some parts of the west of Scotland. The songs and chants unearthed by the programme were perhaps the most revealing. One, sung with gusto by women of the Orange Order to the tune of 'Chirpy, Chirpy, Cheep, Cheep', went: 'Last night I saw my daddy making a bomb. Woke up this morning and the chapel was gone.'

There was also a charming ditty about IRA hunger striker Bobby Sands. To the tune of 'We'll be coming round the mountain' it went:

Could ye go a chicken supper, Bobby Sands
Could ye go a chicken supper,
You dirty Fenian fucker
Could ye go a chicken supper, Bobby Sands

Would ye like a can of Coke, Bobby Sands
Would ye like a can of Coke
I hope you fucking choke
Would ye like a can of coke, Bobby Sands

1995

Orange delight

The Orange Lodge was over the moon with its new phone number when it moved to new offices in Glasgow. The number was (0141–400) 1690. Amazingly, it was chosen at random from thousands of alternative configurations.

The phone company, Atlantic Telecom, was completely unaware that 1690 was the date of the Battle of the Boyne, at which King William of Orange had a famous victory over a Catholic army. A spokesman for the company said he was dumbfounded. But Jack Ramsay – Grand Secretary of the Grand Orange Lodge of Scotland – was delighted and said it would help Orangemen to get to know the new number quickly.

1997

Underhand undertaker

The goings-on at a Glasgow funeral parlour shocked the normally staid world of undertaking. Staff at Wilson's Funeral Services told of the amazing antics of Alex Gallagher, a man who appeared to hate Protestants even if they were dead. He routinely slapped Protestant corpses in the face and said to one corpse, 'You Orange bastard. You'll never walk again.'

Gallagher's behaviour was outrageous in other ways. It was alleged by his colleagues that he:

- Joked about having sex with dead bodies.
- Put his leg over the side of a coffin as if to get in.
- When staff had difficulty in putting a dress on an overweight woman's corpse he called her a 'fat bastard', ripped the dress up the back and laid it on top of her.
- Undid his flies and made a crude remark about a corpse.
- Let staff handle HIV-infected bodies without telling them.
- Tried to get the 'knickers off a girl' in his office who had just lost her baby.
- Boasted that he had sex in the back of a funeral car.

Standards of hygiene also left a lot to be desired. Rats fed on bodies lying on a dirty garage floor. Blood from embalmed corpses was poured down public drains and dogs fed on it as it bubbled up from blocked sewers.

A year after these revelations came out, Wilson's Funeral Services went into liquidation.

1996

Bigoted nurse booted out

Nurse Steve Jamieson's bedside manner left a lot to be desired. While he was temporarily in charge in 1997, Jamieson ruled the Ballantrae ward at Ailsa hospital in Ayr by fear. He fulminated about 'blacks, papes and poofs', described Catholics as scum and intimidated nurses, care assistants and mental patients. It was revealed that he frogmarched fearful patients around the hospital with their arms twisted behind their backs, knelt on a 75-year-old man's chest for thirty minutes and brandished a bread knife.

In another incident Jamieson, from Drongan in Ayrshire, ignored a patient's request to go camping on Arran but he used the patient's treats fund to take the man on a day trip to Belfast, spending time in the Rangers shop on Shankill Road. When Jamieson was asked by colleague James Murphy for his opinion on the progress of a student nurse, Jamieson replied: 'OK, apart from the acrobat around her neck', referring to the woman's crucifix.

He was found guilty of misconduct 'by using excessive force, being aggressive and abusive to patients'. Liz McAnulty, of the UK Central Council of nursing said: 'His behaviour was totally unacceptable from anyone, let alone a registered nurse. . . . He has been removed from the register to protect the public.' Jamieson, who now cannot work as a registered nurse in the United Kingdom, did not attend the hearing and claimed he had been 'stitched up' by his former workmates.

2002

13

It's official – you're numpties

When they are not off sick with 'stress', or at race-awareness seminars, public-sector employees (I almost said workers!) take some very baffling decisions.

The sad vigil of Jimmy the lollipop man

Lollipop man Jimmy Kelly was dedicated to the welfare of children. The only problem was that the school he was responsible for patrolling had been closed for three years. But despite shutting down Park primary school (in the Charing Cross area) barmy bosses at Glasgow City Council refused to give him a new pitch.

So come rain, sleet or snow Jimmy travelled the two miles from his home in Dennistoun to stand outside the deserted school, now converted into flats. He was paid in full for 'working' seventeen hours a week despite the fact that only a handful of kids crossed the road at that point on their way to other schools.

Jimmy was well aware of the irony: 'You could say I feel daft. There's a few kids in the morning but the rest of the day I just put my pole down and wait till it's time to leave. I get some awful abuse from office workers but I'm only doing the job I'm told to.'

Office workers in the area felt sorry for old Jimmy. One said, 'Some of the women in the office wave at him during the day to cheer him up. He never looks happy but then, who would, standing out in the cold all day?'

1999

Nutty head back in the classroom

A head teacher declared insane by a court was given her job back. Muriel MacDonald (35) had faced very serious charges in Stornoway Sheriff Court:

- Drink driving
- Driving her car at a policeman after refusing to stop
- Driving on the wrong side of the road at sixty miles-per-hour, forcing pedestrians to flee

She pleaded guilty to the charges but her lawyers argued that she was temporarily insane. The Crown accepted the testimony of two eminent psychiatrists and she was acquitted. Following treatment at a hospital in Inverness, MacDonald insisted on going back to work. To the dismay of many parents, she was then reinstated to her job as head of a tiny school on the island of Lewis.

1997

Bungling bureaucrats should be certified

For your wife to die of cancer is bad enough. But how would you feel if your wife's former employers sent her a certificate of good attendance a year after she passed away? That is what happened to Robert Wright of Motherwell who lost wife Elizabeth, a school cook, in February 2003.

In April 2004 bungling bureaucrats at North Lanarkshire Council sent out a letter and a gold-star certificate praising her perfect attendance during 2003. The letter – from community services boss, Paul Jukes – said: 'While I recognise that ill health is, in most cases, unavoidable I also appreciate the commitment and dedication necessary to achieve a sickness-free record for a 12-month period.'

The council's insensitivity left hubby Robert in tears. He

had to take four months off work after his wife's death and was still struggling to come to terms with it. 'It makes me sick' he said, 'I thought I had got used to dealing with mail arriving for Liz but this has really shocked me.'

2004

A lady who lunched

As their plane circled the airport for more than half an hour, the fifty-five passengers on board began to speculate about the reasons for the delay in landing. Many people – among them nervous flyers – were afraid that something had gone badly wrong. Others were simply annoyed that a flight already delayed by an electrical fault was going to be even later.

But the real reason the Glasgow to Benbecula flight was still in the air was that an air-traffic controller was finishing her lunch. Meryl Davies was following Civil Aviation Authority guidelines that she could not work for more than two hours without a break. And there was only one controller on duty at the tiny airport in the Western Isles, which has only ten flights a day.

Because of the delay in the aircraft leaving Glasgow her lunch break at 12.30 p.m. coincided with the rearranged landing time. Eventually Meryl returned to her radar screen and the plane landed, fifty-five minutes late.

Hope you enjoyed your piece, Meryl.

1999

How many teachers does it take . . . ?

Highland Council followed its health and safety rules to the letter . . . and paid an electrician from Fort William £144 for a two-hour return trip (including the Corran ferry crossing) to replace two striplights at tiny Ardgour primary school. Apparently janitors and teachers are barred from changing bulbs because it is classified as 'maintenance work'.

The regulations state that only a council-approved electrician could do the job, and no Ardgour-based contractors were on the list because public liability insurance of £5 million is required. Although a local electrician would have charged only £30, the expensive premium ruled out small firms on the island. Angry councillors wanted the rules changed but a spokesman said that, if someone without appropriate insurance cover wrongly wired up a school and it burned down, the council's insurance policy would not be valid.

2002

They're not coffin up

The activities of Edinburgh's new-style traffic wardens have caused great anger among residents of the capital. They are employed by Central Parking System, the company contracted by the City Council to regulate parking. Now known as the Enforcers, they have been high profile . . . to say the least:

- Enforcers overstepped the mark when they ticketed a hearse on double-yellow lines outside McKenzie & Millar, funeral directors, in Great Junction Street, Leith. The outraged undertakers pointed out that the hearse was parked outside their office awaiting a coffin and flower arrangement, and that the firm has parked in the same spot for over a hundred years. Regional manager Philip Spencer said issuing the ticket was unnecessary and insensitive, adding that they would have to carry the coffin down the street if the hearse parked elsewhere. The company intended to fight the £60 fixed-penalty fine in the courts. An AA spokesman confirmed that hearses taking part in a funeral were exempt from parking restrictions and commented: 'Stories like this don't help the image of [parking] attendants.'
- Enforcers plastered a burnt-out car with tickets. The car had been dumped, set on fire and was a wreck with no tyres or windows. Central Parking System later blamed the error on a new recruit.
- An Enforcer told a Kirk minister trying to mediate in a dispute to 'fuck off'. Revd Peter Hadden was trying to help three Americans who were having their hire car towed away on George Street. They had put a pay-and-display sticker on the windscreen but had unwittingly parked in a residents-only bay, which led to the Enforcer calling in a tow-truck. When the subsequent row between the tourists and the Enforcer (assisted by two company supervisors) threatened to take a violent turn, the minister intervened. He was shocked by the attitude of the warden and said 'the air was beginning to turn blue'. His Good Samaritan efforts were to no avail; the car was towed to a compound in Leith and the unhappy Yanks had to pay a £135 towing fine to get it back.

2003

Getting right up our noses

Convicted crack-cocaine dealer and illegal immigrant Althea Matthan (25) was given an £86 return-rail-ticket by hard-up Perth & Kinross Council – to go on holiday. Amazingly, unemployed Matthan was given the taxpayers money so 'she could visit relatives in London' and was also allowed special leave to miss signing-on the dole.

Matthan, a Jamaican national who arrived in Britain illegally in 1991, had been jailed for three years for drug dealing and gave birth to her daughter Crystal while she was inside. She was allowed to stay in Britain while fighting both a Home Office deportation order and a custody battle for her other daughter, 8-year-old Fiona. Although usually impossible for illegal immigrants, Matthan was allocated a rent-free fully furnished council house in Crieff by Perth and Kinross Council, apparently because of baby Crystal. Billy Osborne, who had custody of Fiona, said: 'Matthan's been given the best of houses and then they pay for her to go on holiday as well. It seems that if you sell drugs you will be well looked after by the council.'

In 2002, Matthan was granted legal aid to fight the deportation case on the grounds that she was 'suffering from Aids'. She claimed that treatment in Jamaica was ineffective and suggested that this should allow her leave to remain in Britain.

2001

Sheer loo-nacy

The Scottish Hydro-electric company went overboard when they sent a cheery letter to a toilet in the Highlands! It read 'Welcome to your new home' and was addressed to 'The Occupier, Public Convenience, Newtonmore, Inverness-shire'. An embarrassed official admitted they thought there was a new customer resident at the premises.

1999

Beeb goes Laa-Laa over Teletubby togs

The BBC threatened to sue a tiny community group in Hawick when it was discovered it had supplied Teletubby costumes for children's parties. In a strongly worded letter, television bosses accused Hawick Traditionalists' Association of breach of copyright, pointing out that a licence had not been issued for the use of the costumes. Cancellation of all future events was demanded. Former councillor George Turnbull replied, telling the Beeb killjoys that no money had been made from the free community events, which were put on for the enjoyment of local children.

Five years later, as part of the Tory campaign for the elections to the Scottish Parliament in 2003, the Yellow M advertising agency came up with a poster featuring former leader of the Scottish National Party, Alex Salmond, as Laa-Laa from the Teletubbies. Salmond was referred to as coming from Scot-laa-laa-land but the BBC was not impressed and announced rather stuffily that they were 'the licensor and guardians of the character in conjunction with Rag Doll productions'. The Tories had to withdraw the poster, but had the last laugh: it was estimated that the publicity associated with the stushie would have cost £200,000, just slightly less than the party's entire budget for the election.

1998 and 2003

Student union stabbed Tyson in the back

Despite dripping blood from a stomach wound inflicted by a vicious thug, stab victim Tyson Bennett was refused admission to his student union – because he didn't have his union card with him. The burly doorman at Aberdeen University student union on the city's Gallowgate also stopped Tyson's friend Paul McLune, who did have his membership card, when he tried to get in and phone an ambulance.

Paul and Tyson were told to go down the street to find a telephone box. The pair eventually staggered to a pub where Tyson's wound was bandaged and an ambulance was called. Tyson had to be given twelve stitches and he described the bouncer's behaviour as 'disgraceful'.

1995

Grave error

A funeral turned into a farce when the coffin wouldn't fit into the grave. Eight pallbearers repeatedly tried to lower Mrs Jamesina Green's coffin at Grove cemetery in Aberdeen, but it jammed on the sides of the trench. When cemetery workers tried to free the coffin, lid bolts were wrenched off and horrified mourners thought the body would drop out of the box. Mrs Green was described as a 'large, jolly woman who was extremely well liked' (in other words, she was clinically obese). Many of the funeral guests left, but some remained to watch the successful burial an hour later, once the grave had been widened.

Following the disastrous interment, the family announced that they were refusing to pay Aberdeen District Council's £1,000 bill. The minister who conducted the ceremony, Revd Michael Crawford, said: 'The grave was simply too narrow for the coffin . . . I've never known anything like this.' A cemetery official said that staff had not been informed of the size of the coffin, which he said was 'unusually large and wide'.

1992

Up your kilt

A Partick man was banned from Glasgow's Mitchell Library for being a true Scot and wearing nothing under his kilt.

The problem arose when David McIsaac (63) bent down to pick up notepaper for a disabled friend. Staff in the library got an eyeful as he unwittingly revealed his meat and two veg.

David was indignant at the ban: 'Knickers to them' he bellowed. 'My civil rights are being violated and I'm prepared to take my case to the European Court of Human Rights.'

1993

The oldest schoolboy in Scotland

Brandon Lee had only one ambition in life: to become a doctor. So he took on five Highers in the sixth form at Bearsden Academy and buckled down to work. But there was only one slight problem. He was a 32-year-old university dropout pretending to be just 17. Nor was Brandon Lee his real name; he was in fact Brian MacKinnon, a former pupil at the school who had left more than a decade before.

MacKinnon told his fellow pupils that he was from Canada and his parents were dead, claiming he lived with his granny and had missed out on education while he travelled the world. His classmates thought MacKinnon looked a lot older than he claimed and were suspicious. But his former teachers failed to see through his ruse for the entire academic year.

Although he studied hard and kept to himself, MacKinnon served on the school's student council and reluctantly took part in a school show. Described by classmates as a genius, he got five A-grades in his Highers and was accepted to study medicine at Dundee University. However, the devious Peter Pan was finally unmasked when he went on holiday to Tenerife with fellow pupils. Following a disturbance in a bar, MacKinnon was arrested and two girls discovered that he had two passports; one giving his age as 32, the other stating he was 17.

When the scandal broke, Norman McLeod, rector of the 1300-pupil academy, announced that an investigation was underway. Education chiefs described the case as 'bizarre and baffling'. Although MacKinnon could have returned to school as an adult learner, Dundee University said that it was highly unusual for them to accept anyone aged over 30 and added that they were also investigating.

MacKinnon spent a week keeping a low profile in London before returning home to his mum, who was desperate for him to become a doctor and thought that he had gone back to Bearsden Academy as a mature student. MacKinnon later revealed that he returned to education because he had been forced to abandon medicine at Glasgow University in the early 1980s after a long illness, and he felt cheated. He lost a lot of weight during the illness and his stature had remained that of a schoolboy. MacKinnon convinced the school to admit him by showing a fake letter from his father stating he had been tutored in Canada and he claims a senior member of staff accepted him without seeing a birth certificate.

Dundee University was surprised that the unrepentant MacKinnon did not offer to withdraw but, on 28 September 1995, he was booted out of medicine for a second time. Professor Denis McDevitt, of the faculty of medicine, said that he had obtained a place by using false information. MacKinnon said on television: 'I felt it was the right thing to do at the time.'

1995

14

Animal crackers

Scotland is a nation of animal lovers. Although when you read some of the stories in this chapter you may wonder why.

Moth-eaten

When she heard a loud noise like a motorbike engine and a fluttering feeling in her ear, Patricia MacLeod of Bilston, Midlothian assumed it was tinnitus. But the volume and intensity frightened her, causing her and husband Graham to become alarmed. The ordeal went on for four hours then, to her great relief, the noise suddenly stopped.

She went to her doctor the next day, who diagnosed a build-up of wax in the ear. But, four days later, she was having her ears syringed by a nurse when the body of a moth popped out. It was then she realised what had happened. The MacLeods slept with their bedroom window open in summer and, just next to the window, there is a tree that is infested by moths. The insect had crawled into her ear while she lay asleep in bed. It had then taken four hours to die (probably a lifetime for a moth).

The head man at Butterfly Conservation Scotland, Paul Kirkland, was puzzled: 'People always talk about how earwigs got their names, but I've never heard of anyone getting a moth in their ear.' He did have one suggestion: the moth may have been hungry and after Patricia's ear wax: 'There is such a thing as a wax moth which is very small. They live off the wax in beehives.'

Maybe I'll just keep the window closed from now on . . . even in summer.

2003

Not such a cuddly bear

To a 10-year-old boy like Ross Prendergast, the bear from the television advert for Sugar Puffs must have seemed like the ideal playmate. Secure in its compound in the Camperdown wildlife park in Dundee the 500-pound animal appeared docile and cuddly. The centre had closed for the day and, as no one was around, Ross had sneaked in and decided he wanted to make friends with Jeremy (the bear's name, despite the fact it was a female).

But as he edged towards Jeremy with the intention of patting her on the nose the great beast lunged at him through the wire fence surrounding the compound. The bear ripped off his arm and promptly ate it. Ross later insisted that he had not tormented or teased Jeremy: the animal had pounced on him and pulled his arm through the wire. But the bear had a history of attacks on humans; a few months before it had bitten a zookeeper.

1986

Flock off

Uist crofters went on holiday with their sheep by taking advantage of a Caledonian MacBrayne discount scheme allowing farmers to go to market at a reduced rate. For £29 per person, plus £2.35 per

animal, farmers from islands including Colonsay, Mull, Tiree, South Uist and Barra could travel to Oban market. Cash-strapped crofters welcomed the special offer, which worked out cheaper than standard passenger charges.

But some crafty Uist crofters took sheep to Oban in their cars and left the animals with friends before going on shopping trips or holidays to Glasgow, Edinburgh or Inverness. Cal-Mac's commercial director Ken Duerden said that ferry staff spotted sheep going on holiday and a crofter explained that the sheep returned to the island with the excuse that the price was so low the animals could not be sold. Cal-Mac spokesman Stewart Riddell announced that because of abuse from a small number of people, the scheme was under review.

1998

Sex-crazed jumbo thought keeper was love rival

The thought processes of animals are unfathomable to mere mortals, even when a human has known the beast all its life. So it proved for zookeeper Douglas Robertson (37) who was gored to death by Ben, a three-ton bull elephant he had looked after from birth.

Douglas made the fatal mistake of walking into Ben's enclosure just as he was in the middle of a romp with female jumbo, Kenya. Thinking that the keeper was likely to displace him in Kenya's affections, Ben charged Douglas and knocked him to the ground. When the hapless keeper tried to get up, the 12-year-old pachyderm brutally gored him with razor-sharp tusks. Dozens of families who were visiting the Savage World safari park in Deigne, Belgium looked on, horrified.

Although zoo staff tried to effect a rescue they could not reach Douglas for several hours as Ben and Kenya stood over him. By the time they were able to get him out of the enclosure it was too late and the keeper died in hospital just five hours later.

The tragedy was made yet more poignant by Douglas Robertson's lifelong love of animals. On leaving Bannockburn High School, he became a warden at Blair Drummond safari park and then got a job at a zoo in Germany where Ben and Kenya were born. As his heartbroken father, Robert, said, 'He loved those two animals like they were his own children, and they seemed to love him as well.' In a decision that Douglas would surely have approved of, the safari park decided not to destroy Ben and Kenya.

1995

Hell hounds

It was an idyllic scene. Kellie Lynch (11) and her pal were taking two dogs for a walk in the holiday town of Dunoon. On holiday, Kellie was staying at the Cot House Inn and had made friends with the Rottweilers – called Cassie and Jodie – owned by hotelier, Brian Simpson. During the walk, as they approached a gravel pit, Kellie announced she needed to go to the toilet and handed the chains to her companion. But the dogs dragged her friend towards Kellie and started to lick her face. This caused Kellie to giggle and, for some reason, her laughs enraged the Rottweilers which started to attack her.

As she screamed 'help me', the dogs became frenzied. Her pal kicked the dogs and even lay down in front of Kellie to protect her. But they jumped over her to get at Kellie and, in a savage attack, tore her throat out.

A woman who was passing saw what had happened and started screaming. The dogs lunged at her too but, luckily, owner Brian Simpson arrived on the scene and hit the dogs which then stopped attacking her. The dogs were put down later that day, along with two others that Simpson owned.

The police surgeon who later examined Kellie said he had never seen injuries like it. As well as the horrific damage to her throat the animals had also broken her neck. An animal psychologist, trying to explain the incident, believed that the dogs may have felt threatened by Kellie moving away from them or by her giggling.

This was one of many examples in the late 1980s of people being attacked by Rottweilers and pit bull terriers. Many people called for the law to be changed to make it compulsory for dangerous dogs to be muzzled, including Kellie's mother, Veronica Lynch. Indeed such was her profile that she received many poison-pen letters from so-called dog lovers. And, in a bizarre twist, Kellie's headstone in a Dundee cemetery was vandalised and a man was convicted of stealing flowers from the graveside. As for Brian Simpson he committed suicide six months later after disappearing from his hotel and leaving behind a trail of debts.

1989

'Yogi must stay'

Scotland is a nation of animal lovers . . . even when the animal is dead. This was made crystal clear to John Stewart of Ike's Pizza Emporium in Edinburgh. To amuse his customers John put a stuffed bear – known, inevitably, as Yogi – outside the restaurant. Yogi talked to the customers thanks to a loudspeaker wired to his mouth and, at Christmas, he dressed up as Santa 'Claws'.

But he reckoned without the animal rights' brigade. Nina Smith, of Advocates for Animals, wrote to him in no uncertain terms. 'I am writing to inform you of the extreme distaste which I have for the real stuffed bear you feel moved to exhibit outside your pizza restaurant.' She was backed up by Libearty, the worldwide campaign for bears.

But John organised a petition of traders and tourists and their message was clear: Yogi must stay! John blasted back: 'These people should keep their paws off Yogi. I inherited him when I took over the restaurant . . . and the previous owner told me he died of natural causes. I will definitely be keeping him. He is very popular with customers.'

1993

Bertie's big day out

The roughnecks on the Beatrice Alpha oil rig are well used to visitors descending from the sky in helicopters. They even get the odd racing pigeon. But never tiny, caged birds. So imagine their surprise when a budgie dropped in on their rig 12 miles off the Caithness coast.

The intrepid budgerigar – who they promptly nicknamed Bertie – had escaped from its home in Wick and flown boldly where no budgie has flown before. Bob Milne, an animal-welfare officer from Aberdeen, reckoned the bird had been blown off course by strong winds. Bob thought Bertie was lucky; after all, who knows where it might have ended up if it had not found the rig.

But all's well that ends well. The men of Beatrice Alpha took Bertie under their wing and the budgie was sent back VIP-style in a helicopter to Bob Milne's home in Aberdeen. Fortunately the bird was identified by the ring number on its leg and was soon reunited with owner Perry Campbell and 3-year-old daughter, Stacey. Appropriately enough, they revealed that the bird's real name was Lucky.

1993

Goldfish supper

Some diners at the Insomnia restaurant in Glasgow obviously hadn't had enough to eat . . . because they scoffed live goldfish from the ornamental bathtub.

A local aquarium supplied the fish and the owner explained: 'We've put forty fish in it and within weeks they were all dead. I've pulled ashtrays, cigarettes and tumblers out of the tub. There have been dead fish lying there for days at a time.' He said he had complained several times about abuse of the fish.

The owners of the restaurant said the fish had either been

eaten or thrown about. 'When you have drunken people it's not easy to control.' The SSPCA promised to investigate.

1996

Salty sealed his permit

Salty the seal was threatened with execution at dawn for allegedly guzzling thousands of pounds worth of precious salmon stocks. He had become trapped in shallow water in the river Leven when his attempt to reach the sea after a stay in Loch Lomond failed. However, hundreds of locals turned out in protest and the execution was suspended on condition that the hungry seal was removed from the river.

While the rescue attempt continued, Salty's poaching activities were finally legalised by exasperated Loch Lomond Angling Improvement Association officials who gave him an interim fishing permit worth £150, complete with a passport-sized photograph! Association chairman Michael Brady said that Salty (also known as Houdini) might have had trouble defending himself in court, despite his strong personality. The permit stated that Sunday fishing was prohibited so Salty was still at risk from prosecution. Fortunately, the following week, the slippery customer made it over the weir into Loch Lomond and promptly disappeared.

2003

Frozen chicken laid an egg

When Rod Sloan found Beatrice, a bantam chicken, with her feet frozen to the ground outside his home in Inverurie, Aberdeenshire he quickly organised a rescue using some unusual tools. The poor hen, which weighs only a pound and was near to death, was warmed up with his daughter Katie's hairdryer and then carefully prized loose with a penknife. The harassed hen then laid an egg in panic! The tale has a happy ending as Beatrice was nursed back to health by 12-year-old Katie.

2003

Bee-sieged

Lisa and Stuart Grant of Freuchie were surprised when a neighbour called at their home on a Sunday afternoon and told them that their chimney-stack was coated in bees. Lisa (26) said that the chimney-stack looked like it was covered in fur. Then, as thousands of angry bees got into the kitchen and a spare room, Stuart (28) phoned for help. No-one was prepared to help on a Sunday so the Fife couple had to use bin-bags to block vents as they beat a hasty retreat to the lounge. Lisa said: 'We couldn't hear the TV for the buzzing.' However, pest-control experts arrived the following day, the crazed insects were smoked out and the Grant household returned to normal.

2001

Puss in boats

An adventurous cat – appropriately named Nelson – took to life on the ocean wave and sailed back to his birthplace by stowing away on an Orkney inter-island ferry! The six-month-old tabby had mysteriously vanished from his house in Kirkwall on Orkney's Mainland. His new owner, Gary Carter (10), was very worried until Nelson turned up safely near the home of his former owner, Fiona Thompson, on Westray.

The homesick cat's amazing journey began when glaziers called to do a job for the Carters. As they left, Nelson hid in their van and travelled over the sea to Westray with them. When Nelson's disappearance was noticed, Gary's mum, Liz, phoned the glaziers to find where the van was going next – then called folk on Westray to look out for the missing moggie.

1998

Snakes alive!

Viper mad Nigel Carruthers kept thirty-one snakes out of sight in his bedroom, so that they didn't frighten visitors. Soon after he married Trish in 1990 she was persuaded to keep the pet collection in the bedroom of their house on Orkney's Mainland. By 1997, there was a 9-feet-long python, two adult boa constrictors with twenty-three babies, three corn snakes and two milk snakes.

To complete the menagerie there was also a food supply consisting of 150 caged rats, and a freezer full of 500 frozen ones, just in case the snakes felt like a snack. Nigel (34), who had been disabled by a back injury, said that none of his snakes were poisonous and he reckoned that his wife deserved a medal for putting up with his private zoo. Trish (44) said that she wasn't too bothered about the creepy collection and added that it didn't affect her love life.

1997

Udder madness

Deeside Gliding Club was awarded £50,000 by the National Lottery fund to stop cows licking their gliders. The cows graze on the airstrip in Dinnet, Aberdeenshire but they developed a preference for the weatherproof paint that coats the gliders, and the beasts spent hours licking the aircraft instead of nibbling the grass.

Pilots, who wasted hours scraping off the goo left by the slavering cattle, asked the National Lottery for £50,000 towards the cost of a hangar so that planes could be kept indoors and away from the addicted bovines. Club secretary Jim Davidson was pleased to receive the money for a 'badly-needed facility' and said: 'We are more than happy to share our home with the animals. But whenever they're grazing at night, they do tend to take a fancy to our aircraft.'

1995

Highland cow kills pensioner

A pensioner died after he was butted and tossed into the air by an angry Highland cow with a calf. Brian Williams (74), from St

Albans in Hertfordshire, was walking with his family on a private road in the Inverinate estate in Inverness-shire when the incident occurred. He said the impact felt like going three rounds with Cassius Clay but later became unconscious during the drive back to the family's rented cottage in Plockton. After being taken by road to Broadford hospital on Skye, Mr Williams was airlifted to the Southern General in Glasgow where he died from a brain haemorrhage. He was taking the blood-thinning drug Warfarin for a heart condition and it is thought this may have been a contributory factor in his death.

The chairman of Plockton community council, Charlie MacRae, rejected the family's suggestions that more could have been done to warn visitors of the dangers presented by the cows. He said: 'Cows have roamed free for more than 100 years and there have been no other serious incidents.'

2003

Cyber cemetery

Euilleam Ross, of Invergordon in Easter Ross, opened Scotland's first internet cemetery for animals. At £199 to rent a make-believe space on a computer it was certainly not cheap. But barking-mad punters could 'put' a memorial plot, a headstone or a mausoleum anywhere: their favourite beauty spot; an Orkney stone circle; or even on the top of Ben Nevis.

Grieving customers picked an image of their favourite place then chose a monument and a garden of remembrance. A picture of the deceased pet and a short eulogy could also be added. Euilleam (67) said that his cyber graveyard featured a wide range of pets, including parrots, hamsters and spiders.

2000

15

We are not amused

The tide of permissiveness has well and truly reached the shore. Theatres, newspapers and television are all in danger of drowning.

She was left fuming

Circus performer Bebe Rose had a shock show-stopper. She poured petrol into her private parts and set it alight. But it all went horribly wrong during a performance at the Edinburgh Fringe when it leaked out and dribbled down her thighs. When she ignited the gasoline it blew up and Bebe was left with burns on her legs.

The Frenchwoman blamed it on the petrol she had bought at a local filling station. She explained that the flames are meant to go out when they come in contact with the skin, but apparently Scottish petrol is more combustible – something she learned the hard way.

Bebe had been performing her topless routine for four years in husband Jim Rose's freak-show circus. She intended to give up the act within two years to start a family but reckoned she 'came very close to saying goodbye to that. I am still sore but I consider myself lucky. It could have been much worse.'

1997

The sickest of them all

The murder of sixteen innocent children at a Dunblane primary school in 1996 by fiend Thomas Hamilton shocked the world. So it seems incredible that anyone would want to mock those who were mown down. But that is exactly what happened only twelve months later.

The *Paranoia Monthly* website had a game with smiling children as targets and urged players to 'annihilate all targets in under one minute using 100 bullets or less'. Players were invited to compete for the title of 'fastest gun in Dunblane'.

The game's main character was a revolver-toting gunman. In a clear reference to Hamilton's perverted practices it said: 'A fetish for scantily clad Boy Scouts would also be an advantage.' The promoters clearly had no doubt about their motives and the website boasted it 'reaches depths of depravity other websites cannot reach'.

The game caused outrage. One Dunblane mother, whose daughter was killed by Hamilton, said: 'The people who put this game on the internet must be absolutely sick. It takes a warped mind to dream up a game like this. I'm disgusted.' Virgin Net, which hosted the site, said it would force the people behind *Paranoia Monthly* to remove the game.

1997

Gay Ron got under their skin

The Centre for Contemporary Arts in Glasgow's Sauchiehall Street is no stranger to controversy. Over the years it has done many things that have tested the limits of artistic expression. But a show by self-confessed heroin addict and homosexual activist Ron Athey needled many people.

In the show, Athey, who was HIV positive, stabbed himself with hypodermic needles until he started bleeding. Ron did not believe the audience would be in danger of catching AIDS. 'Lies have been told that I squirt contaminated blood at the audience – it's not true.'

It was certainly popular in some quarters and the show came close to being a sell-out. A spokesman for Glasgow District Council said: 'We believe the public should make up their own minds.'

1995

They weren't Buchan interested

It was a noble ambition. To take culture to those parts of Scotland which often miss out. So when the world-renowned Vienna Festival Ballet planned to put on a production of *Swan Lake* in Peterhead, Buchan, there was much licking of lips by local culture-vultures.

Theatre bosses were confident that people would be trampled in the rush for tickets. But they soon discovered that the good burghers of the sleepy fishing town were distinctly underwhelmed. Only two tickets were sold for the matinee and just four for the evening performance. The ballet company immediately pulled out.

It seems there was much more interest in Peterhead's top cultural attraction – the Gala bingo hall, which had punters flocking to enjoy its delights seven nights a week. Or in the hit movie *Lock, Stock and Two Smoking Barrels*, which was showing at a local cinema. Or even the table-top dancers at Drummond's bar. Alex Salmond, the town's MP, admitted that a ballet was not to the taste of locals: '*Swan Lake* just might have been slightly on the highbrow side.'

1998

Not so fandabidozi

It is almost like a badge of honour for showbiz celebrities when they get their own official stalker. So tacky variety act the Krankies (career high-point *Crackerjack*) must have thought they had finally made it when 'Jimmy Krankie' (actress Janette Tough) was stalked by a sick lesbian midget. The 22-year-old stalker:

- Begged the Krankies to let her live with them
- Sent letters threatening to kill them
- Hitchhiked all over Britain to see their act
- Tracked down family members in the west of Scotland to get information on their childhood

The stalker lived with her parents in Derby and the duo (Janette and husband Ian Tough) had complained to police about her. 'Jimmy' said that her tiny tormentor was like an emotional basket-case: 'The girl is very small like me. She started writing for advice and then declaring her love. But she quickly became twisted and confused, wanting to live with me one minute and kill me the next.'

After all that, even the working men's club in Cumnock, or panto in Falkirk, might be appealing.

1993

They didn't hail taxi play

Playwright James O'Brien was denounced by Ulster politicians from both sides of the religious divide for *Butchers*, an account of vicious sectarian murders in Belfast. Mirroring real life, the play began with the audience of thirty being abducted and driven away in black taxis to a secret basement venue. Ulster Unionist MP Ken Maginnis described the play at the Edinburgh Festival Fringe as 'absolutely sick' while the nationalist MP for West Belfast, Dr Joe Hendron, said he was 'deeply disturbed'.

The play was based on the vile activities of the Shankill Butchers gang which, between 1972 and 1977, reputedly killed more people than any other mass murderers in British history. Led by Lennie Murphy, the gang selected dozens of mainly Catholic victims and dragged them to dark alleys or cellars for hours of torture and mutilation, before beating them to death or hacking them to bits using butchers' knives, axes, swords or machetes. It is known that some of the victims were kidnapped from Catholic ghettos in black taxis. Although some gang members were prosecuted, Murphy was not convicted of murder; but the IRA dispensed its own brand of justice and killed him in a hail of bullets in 1982.

Mr O'Brien insisted he had no wish to offend anyone and

said that kidnapping the audience was 'a device to heighten dramatic tension'. He described the play as 'a piece about the nature of evil' and blithely added: 'The point about taking the audience away by taxi is to disorientate them and take them away from the idea of a night out at the theatre. My main concern is not to trivialise the issue.'

The play was booked for six nights at Edinburgh's controversial Richard Demarco Gallery.

1992

Off with his head

There was outrage when photographer Joel-Peter Witkin (55) put on a vile and disturbing photo exhibition in Edinburgh's Stills Gallery. It featured chopped-up bodies, a severed head and a man with breasts. Rent-a-quote Tory MP Phil Gallie said: 'It is pornography. I want the arts minister to get it banned.' An unrepentant Witkin said: 'I aim to show sublime beauty in darkness.'

The New Yorker, whose 'art' has been described as an 'intellectually camouflaged freak show' revealed that, as a youngster, he had witnessed the decapitation of a little girl in a horrific car accident; the girl's head rolled to his feet. A spokeswoman for the Arts Council-funded gallery suggested critics should visit the exhibition before condemning it.

1995

Fancy a nibble?

Protestors objected to *Appetite*, an Edinburgh Fringe show that featured gratuitous lesbian sexual activity. Any claim that bouncy trapeze troupe Club Swing were interested in art rather than porn rang hollow when it was announced that the quartet of Australian dykes charged punters £7.50 to nibble strawberries, apples and cream cakes from their bodies. Anni Davey, Kathryn

Niesche, Simone O'Brien and Celia White also simulated oral sex and masturbation as they swung around in the altogether; in a former church, of all places. They also appeared in corsets, cycle shorts and kinky boots.

Promoter Douglas Hunter argued that *Appetite* was simply erotic rather than pornographic. But Moira Knox, a Tory councillor, said the show was highly indecent, condemned it as a 'dirty-minded disgrace' and called for the procurator fiscal to issue a ban. The Fringe was also attacked as a 'highly commercial' parasite living off the back of the city's famous International Festival and Ms Knox added that the trapeze production appealed 'only to the lowest part of people's minds'.

Predictably Club Swing used the 'dirty-minded disgrace' slogan on its publicity posters and the crowds rolled in. A gushing arts critic at the *Glasgow Herald* described the show as 'a circus for the 90s . . . thrilling, decadent, a celebration wrapped in canvas'. At the end of the festival, *Appetite* was awarded a 'Moira', the prize for the most outrageous Fringe show.

1995

Virgin on the ridiculous

An exhibit planned for Glasgow's Centre for Contemporary Arts was swiftly removed to avoid upsetting the city's Catholics. The so-called work of art featured a statue of the Virgin Mary covered in a giant condom! Lord Gowrie, chairman of the Arts Council for England (which owns the statue), ordered the withdrawal. The move angered the trend-setting gallery.

1995

Criminal record

Legendary criminal Charles Bronson prepared the sleeve artwork and spoke on the album *Caged*, featuring Edinburgh-based hardcore punk band, the Swellbellys. The feared hardman, who is six-foot tall and weighs 250 pounds, changed his name by deed poll from Michael Peterson in honour of the star of the *Death Wish* vigilante movies. He was jailed for seven years for armed robbery in 1974 but his rooftop-siege and hostage-taking stunts in prison and later violent crimes have earned him a total of twenty-six years in solitary confinement. He has now been in prison continuously since 1993.

Bronson also wrote the lyrics for a track called 'Sucking out the pain', which appeared on another Swellbelly's CD, and he plans to tour with the band following his release, if he ever gets out. His appeal against his life sentence failed in April 2004 but he is due for parole in 2010.

The Swellbellys appeared on a sick video entitled 'Sincerely Yours', which included real-life scenes of Bronson holding hostages. It was banned in August 2000 by Home Secretary Jack Straw.

2000–2004

Cunning stunts included nude nun in a bottle

When the Circus of Horrors planned to visit Aberdeen, many church leaders called for their 'freak show' to be banned. The turns included a contortionist who squeezed into a glass jar, then wriggled out to reveal she was only wearing a nun's head-dress. Other highlights included a man's tongue being nailed to a brick and jugglers tossing chainsaws. There was also a particularly odious act featuring a woman using a firework inserted into her private parts to turn herself into a flame-thrower. A circus spokesman said: 'There's a good chance the audience will see someone get hurt. Naturally, some of the acts will shock.'

2000

It's your funeral

When Jeannie McLennan of Inverness saw the name McLennan in the death notices of the *Highland News*, she wondered if it was someone she knew. But she was horrified to realise it was herself when she read the name 'Jean McLennan née Carter'. The notice gave full details of the 'funeral' arrangements.

The *Highland News* told her that the hoaxer who placed it claimed to be her sister. The surprisingly detailed notice mentioned two of Jeannie's children, and included her father's nickname, Ginger. Funeral director William Fraser was also named in the sick advert. She revealed that she was the victim of a hate campaign and had received threatening phone calls which, despite her going ex-directory, had restarted. During one call a young woman announced that she was 'dead meat'. Then, shortly after the notice appeared, she went to her local supermarket and a shocked worker said to her, 'What are you doing here? You're supposed to be dead.'

The police said they were conducting an investigation into the hate campaign. In view of the upset that had been caused, the editor said the paper would now only accept death notices from undertakers.

But Jeannie was determined not to let the hoaxer win, so she appeared at the 'funeral' on 16 June 2000. Afterwards she said: 'It's not every day you get a chance to attend your own funeral, and it gave me an opportunity to explain to any friends and relatives who unwittingly turned up. It also gave me a chance to come to terms with what happened.'

2000

The boot's on the other foot

The founder of an exclusive health spa and hotel was appalled when she was described as an 'international boot' by toff's magazine, *Tatler*. Gaynor Winyard (67), who ran Stobo Castle, was upset because she knew the meaning of the word 'boot'. *Tatler* also alleged that her son, Stephen Winyard, gave guests 'personalised massages'.

The Winyards sued *Tatler* for libel and her lawyer told the High Court in London that: 'The article meant that . . . Gaynor Winyard was sexually promiscuous. In some parts of the country the word boot means a woman who is promiscuous, a slut, a tart.'

Although the magazine later printed an apology, Mrs Winyard was awarded damages of £75,000 by the court while her son got £15,000.

1990